Edgar Allan Poe

Titles in the series Critical Lives present the work of leading cultural figures of the modern period. Each book explores the life of the artist, writer, philosopher or architect in question and relates it to their major works.

Edgar Allan Poe

Kevin J. Hayes

REAKTION BOOKS

For Hyun-woo and Ji-eun

Published by Reaktion Books Ltd
33 Great Sutton Street
London EC1V ODX, UK
www.reaktionbooks.co.uk

First published 2009

Copyright © Kevin J. Hayes 2009

Printed and bound in Great Britain
by CPI Antony Rowe, Chippenham, Wiltshire

British Library Cataloguing in Publication Data
Hayes, Kevin J.
    Edgar Allan Poe. – (Critical lives)
    1. Poe, Edgar Allan, 1809–1849
    2. Authors, American – 19th century – Biography
    I. Title   II. Series
    818.3'09-dc22

ISBN: 978 1 86189 515 8

Contents

W. S. Hartshorn and C. T. Tatman, *Edgar Allan Poe*, 1904.

Introduction

No American author has influenced the history of literature and the arts more than Edgar Allan Poe. But at the time of his death in 1849, the profound influence of his writings – verse, fiction, and criticism – was by no means assured. In his last few years Poe was known in the US primarily as the author of 'The Raven'. A handful of his short stories were translated into French and Russian in the late 1840s, but not until the following decade would Europe discover his work and recognize his genius. More than anyone, Charles Baudelaire was responsible for celebrating Poe's greatness and disseminating his work. Baudelaire saw Poe as a kindred spirit, someone who had crystallized into prose many ideas he had imagined himself but had yet to articulate. It was Poe's fortune that one of France's greatest poets became his greatest champion. Baudelaire's translations not only helped Poe achieve a level of status in France akin to that of a major national author, they also circulated throughout Europe for decades to come. Overall, Poe's critical reputation took two separate directions after his death. Whereas readers in English-speaking nations hesitated to recognize his genius, European readers accepted him and his works wholeheartedly.

The obituary Rufus Wilmot Griswold published in the *New York Tribune* largely shaped Poe's reputation after his death. Griswold harshly criticized Poe's personal habits, depicting him as a misan-thrope, a mad and melancholy loner, someone who wandered the city streets night and day, alternately mumbling curses or prayers and not much caring which was which. According to Griswold, Poe was devoid of honour, devoid of morality, devoid of any and all elevating personal qualities. Griswold further asserted that Poe's imaginative writings, especially the poems and stories of his final years, were based on personal events. The assertion gave readers licence to understand Poe's stories through his life, his life through his stories. This dual impulse still affects the popular understanding of Poe's life and works. Even now, many readers see his mentally unbalanced narrators as reflections of a disturbed mind, not as products of a rich imagination. Many contemporary readers were shocked by Griswold's obituary, but few doubted its details. His portrayal became the accepted image of Poe in both the US and UK.

Perhaps the strangest aspect of Griswold's scathing obituary is the fact that Poe had chosen him as his literary executor, the one to carry out his final wishes in regard to his writings. Why would Poe choose such a mean-spirited man as his literary executor? Poe's forward-thinking fiction anticipates the future in so many ways: could he not foresee what Griswold would do after his death? Surely Poe must have had some inkling of Griswold's intentions. After all, he had publicly attacked Griswold's popular anthology *The Poets and Poetry of America* numerous times. He had to expect some sort of posthumous payback. But there are reasons to explain why Poe chose Griswold as his literary executor. In the time Poe spent as author and editor, he had learned much about the publishing world. Here's one thing he learned: controversy sells books. And in his dealings with Griswold, he had learned something important about him: Griswold got things done. Poe could be reasonably sure Griswold would edit and publish a posthumous collected edition of his writings. And he did. The first two volumes, which consisted of Poe's short fiction and poetry, appeared together the year after Poe's death. Griswold subsequently edited and published two additional volumes of Poe's miscellaneous writings. To reiterate his opinion of Poe, Griswold republished his obituary as part of the collection's first volume, further disseminating his negative portrayal of Poe's character.

The most substantial review of Griswold's edition appeared in the *Southern Literary Messenger,* the magazine Poe made famous. The article, which appeared anonymously, was written by John M. Daniel.[1] Following Griswold's lead, Daniel reinforced Poe's negative qualities. Though Daniel praised Poe's literary originality, he did so only after depicting him as an immoral, inconsiderate brute. Oblivious to what passes for proper behaviour in polite society, Poe, according to Daniel, said whatever he wished and did whatever he wanted. Poe was someone who could control neither his drinking nor his critical opinions. He took in drink and spewed out criticism without regard to what others thought. He was a cast-off of society, an Ishmaelite, a deviant who went one way when everyone else went the other.

This attitude toward Poe's character presented a barrier to appreciation for American and British readers. Committed to the increasingly antiquated notion that literature should perform a moral function, Anglo-American readers questioned the ultimate value of Poe's work. How can the writings of someone so apparently devoid of morality exert a positive, elevating effect on readers? Robert Louis Stevenson's reaction is typical. In an 1875 essay, Stevenson admitted that Poe had 'the true story-teller's instinct' and appreciated 'The Cask of Amontillado' and 'The Masque of the Red Death', but derided other tales as he critiqued Poe's personality. Stevenson observed: 'I cannot find it in my heart to like either his portrait or his character; and though it is possible that we see him more or less refracted through the strange medium of his works, yet I do fancy that we can direct, alike in these, in his portrait, and the facts of his life . . . a certain jarring note, a taint of something that we do not care to dwell upon or find a name for.'[2]

Clearly, Stevenson let his understanding of Poe's character hinder the enjoyment of his work. In the English-speaking world, Poe's idealistic verse was accepted earlier and more easily than his weird tales.

Continental readers developed a very different attitude toward Poe, though theirs largely stemmed from the same basic information. The scattered stories Baudelaire encountered in the late 1840s first attracted him to Poe, but when he read Daniel's article, he found the figure of Poe enormously appealing. The way Daniel portrayed Poe closely resembled how Baudelaire saw himself. In Baudelaire's eyes, Daniel's depiction of Poe's character was praise, not criticism. He fitted the mould of the *poète maudit* perfectly. Edgar Allan Poe is the bad boy of American literature.

In 1852 Baudelaire published a major biographical and critical essay on Poe. Though he did not admit it, nearly two-thirds of the essay is an almost word-for-word translation from Daniel's article in the *Southern Literary Messenger*.[3] Baudelaire went on to translate many of Poe's short stories as well as his most renowned critical essays. Before his death in 1867, he published five volumes of Poe translations. Oddly, he translated few poems, leaving that task to another major French poet. In 1889 Stéphane Mallarmé issued a substantial collection of Poe's verse in French. The translation would foster the development of Symbolist poetry throughout Europe.

Baudelaire's translation of the short fiction had a profound impact on Poe's reception across France and throughout Europe. Guy de Maupassant used what he learned from reading Poe to perfect his own tales and, in doing so, developed a reputation as the greatest writer of short stories in French. Poe's pioneering tales of science fiction significantly influenced Jules Verne, who also enjoyed Poe's imaginative journeys. He wrote *The Sphinx of the Icefields*, a fanciful tale of polar exploration, as a sequel to Poe's novel, *The Narrative of Arthur Gordon Pym*. Verne even dedicated *The Sphinx of the Icefields* to Poe's memory.

Translations of Poe into other European languages often came second-hand. Instead of being translated from Poe's English, in other words, they were translated from Baudelaire's French. Early Polish translators of Poe, for example, used Baudelaire as their base text.[4] So did the great Russian writer Konstantin Balmont, who published his translation of Poe's tales in 1895. Balmont also translated Poe's verse into Russian, which strongly influenced the Russian Symbolist poets, as well as those working in other art forms.[5] Rakhmaninov's choral symphony *The Bells* is based on Balmont's translation of Poe's similarly titled poem.

Like Baudelaire, major writers in Europe and Latin America found the depiction of Poe as *poète maudit* quite appealing. The great Croatian writer Antun Gustov Matoš saw himself as a tortured artist and identified with Poe closely. Poe's short stories helped shape Matoš's fiction significantly. For one work, Matoš even took his pseudonym from the name of a famous Poe character, 'Hop-Frog'.[6] Nicaraguan poet Rubén Darío identified with Baudelaire's image of Poe, whose bold experimentations in verse set a precedent for Darío's own innovative poetry. Darío also wrote an essay glorifying Poe's accomplishments, depicting him as a misunderstood genius, someone whose brilliance blinded his short-sighted, dull-minded contemporaries.[7]

Poe's influence on the arts extends well beyond the realm of literature. Mallarmé shared his own enthusiasm for Poe with Edouard Manet. In 1875 they collaborated to produce *Le Corbeau*, which consisted of Mallarmé's French translation of 'The Raven' with illustrations by Manet. Mallarmé was also friends with Paul Gauguin, whose portrait of him depicts Mallarmé with a raven on his shoulder. Having read Baudelaire's translations of Poe's tales, Gauguin kept them in mind when he went to the South Pacific. He was moved by the paradox in 'Ligeia', the idea that great beauty requires a certain *'strangeness* in the proportion'. Considering *Woman with a Flower*, which he painted in Tahiti, Gauguin said that the figure's forehead 'with the majesty of upsweeping lines, reminded me of that saying of Poe's, "There is no perfect beauty without a certain singularity in the proportions."' Gauguin was not alone among French painters in his admiration of this idea. Eugène Delacroix had read Baudelaire's translation of 'Ligeia' earlier and copied the same passage from the story into his journal.[8]

The Surrealists found in Poe a kindred spirit, as well. Max Ernst, for one, greatly enjoyed Baudelaire's translations. None of Poe's works affected him more than 'Berenice', which resurfaces in Ernst's collages, paintings and critical writings. Ernst's automatic methods for painting involved a kind of obsessional staring reminiscent of the narrator's behaviour in 'Berenice'. Poe also inspired Salvador Dalí and René Magritte, who created several paintings named after Poe's tales. Poe's influence on painting went beyond Surrealism. To take just one more major painter as an example, Robert Motherwell created a series of Abstract Expressionist collages inspired by Poe's works.[9]

Poe has exerted a similar influence on the cinema, providing subjects for filmmakers, but also influencing the development of cinematic theory and technique. The subject of Poe and the cinema brings to mind those cheesy, low-budget adaptations of the 1960s directed by Roger Corman and starring Vincent Price, but Poe's influence on the cinema is much more pervasive. It stretches back to the days of D. W. Griffith. In honour of the centenary of Poe's birth in 1909, Griffith directed *Edgar Allan Poe*, a brief biopic that incorporates elements of 'The Raven' and other works and thus reinforces the longstanding tradition of reading Poe's works as a reflection of his life. Notably, Griffith makes unprecedented use of chiaroscuro in *Edgar Allan Poe* – unprecedented in the cinema, that is. Poe's short fiction frequently makes use of chiaroscuro and other vivid images of light and shadow. Griffith returned to Poe in 1914 with *The Avenging Conscience*, a feature-length adaptation of 'The Tell-Tale Heart'.

For this tale, Poe created a way to express the profound psychological tension his guilt-ridden narrator feels. Griffith brilliantly replicates Poe's psychological tension in visual terms.

Poe's critical writings also helped shape the development of the cinema. According to his compositional theory, a short story should possess a fundamental unity, all elements working together toward a single effect. This idea resurfaces in late nineteenth-century short-story writing manuals and in other forms of expression. Poe's compositional theory significantly affected Maurice Ravel, for instance. Priding himself on his craftsmanship, Ravel composed his music following Poe's concept of the totality of effect.[10] Poe's critical writings similarly affected the construction of film plots. Emphasizing the idea that all story elements should work toward a single, unified effect, early screenwriting manuals sound remarkably familiar to anyone who has read Poe's criticism.[11]

The tales have continued to provide subject matter for cheesy, low-budget film adaptations, but they have also inspired some of the world's greatest filmmakers. Federico Fellini's feature-length films reflect an audacious absurdity or, perhaps, an absurdist audacity typical of Poe's humorous tales. The leaders of New Wave French cinema greatly respected Poe, too. 'The Oval Portrait' helped inspire the story of Jean-Luc Godard's 1962 film, *Vivre sa Vie*. Toward the end of the film, one character even appears reading Poe's story from a collection of his fiction. And François Truffaut's protagonist in *Fahrenheit 451* is memorizing an edition of Poe as the film ends.

Poe's influence on world literature has persisted through the twentieth century and into the twenty-first. Franz Kafka's expressions of persecution and alienation recall Poe's tales of mystery and imagination. Walter Benjamin better understood the meaning of the modern world after reading 'The Man of the Crowd' and 'The Philosophy of Furniture'. Poe's writings have greatly influenced several major Latin American authors. Jorge Luis Borges appreciated

Poe's imaginative powers, his quest for originality and his ability to create works that transcended the times in which he wrote them. Argentine novelist Julio Cortázar first read Poe's tales as a child and returned to them throughout his literary career. Like Poe, Cortázar recognized the power of dreams as both a source of inspiration and a mode of expression.[12] And Mexican novelist Carlos Fuentes has filled his fiction with imagery eerily reminiscent of Poe's.

In light of Edgar Allan Poe's impact on the history of literature and the arts, his life deserves another look. From the late 1820s through the next two decades, he created some of the finest short stories, some of the most memorable poetry and some of the most insightful and perceptive criticism ever written. The amazing thing is that he did all this in the face of abject poverty. Though he lived much of his adult life in squalor, he never turned his back on literature, never compromised his art for the sake of commercial gain. In a letter he wrote to one publisher early in his literary career, Poe used the language of the marriage ceremony to express his dedication to the world of literature. His was a pitiful life in many ways, but Poe's commitment to literature is awe-inspiring.

1

The Contest

Learning the outcome of an 1833 literary contest sponsored by the Baltimore *Saturday Visiter*, Edgar Allan Poe received the news that October with mixed feelings. He was thrilled one of his entries, 'Manuscript Found in a Bottle', had won the fiction contest but disappointed that another, a contemplative poem in blank verse titled 'The Coliseum', had lost the poetry contest. Always a fierce competitor, Poe took defeat hard. The judges had chosen 'The Coliseum' as the best poem, but once they awarded 'Manuscript Found in a Bottle' the fiction prize, they gave the poetry prize to the author of 'The Song of the Winds', an unknown Baltimore poet named Henry Wilton. Poe's disappointment turned to anger when he learned 'Henry Wilton' was the pen name of John Hill Hewitt, the editor of the *Visiter*. How could a magazine's editor win a contest sponsored by its publisher?

Soon after the winning entries appeared, Poe headed to the *Visiter* office at the corner of Baltimore and Gay, where he caught up with Hewitt as he was about to enter. Poe scowled ominously.[1]

'You have used underhanded means, sir, to obtain that prize over me,' Poe said sternly.

'I deny it, sir,' Hewitt replied.

'Then why did you keep back your real name?'

'I had my reasons,' Hewitt told him, 'and you have no right to question me.'

'But you tampered with the committee, sir,' Poe insisted.

'The committee are gentlemen above being tampered with, sir; and if you say that you insult them,' Hewitt responded, looking Poe in the eye.

'I agree that the committee are gentlemen,' Poe said, 'but I cannot place *you* in that category.' As Hewitt told the story, Poe's dark eyes now flashed with fury.

Hearing these sharp words, the quick-tempered Hewitt could no longer control himself. He struck Poe, who staggered back but remained on his feet. Happily, passing friends stopped the quarrel before one man could challenge the other to a duel.

Though the contest had provoked Poe's ire, his trouble with Hewitt went much deeper and involved Lambert A. Wilmer, who had come to Baltimore to edit the *Visiter*. Wilmer had reached a professional agreement with Charles F. Cloud, the magazine's proprietor. Cloud would supply the capital, and Wilmer would invest his time and editorial expertise. The two would share profits equally. At this time editing periodicals remained largely an amateur pursuit, an endeavour undertaken by those with other means of support. Wilmer's arrangement marks a groundbreaking step toward professional editing.[2]

When Cloud established the *Visiter*, its main competition was the *Baltimore Minerva*, which Hewitt, a composer and music teacher, edited part-time. Under Wilmer's leadership, the *Visiter* succeeded, forcing the *Minerva* out of business. Hewitt approached Cloud next, offering to edit the *Visiter* for nothing. Cloud accepted the offer and dismissed Wilmer. Whereas Wilmer was trying to make journalism a serious profession, Hewitt's actions reverted it to an amateur pursuit. Wilmer successfully sued Cloud for breach of contract.

Hewitt's dilettantish attitude toward editing underlies Poe's dispute with him. Poe sympathized with Wilmer's efforts to turn journalism into a bona fide profession. By this time – he was twenty-four – Poe had decided to devote his life to literature and hoped to edit a magazine himself someday – someday soon perhaps. That Hewitt had entered a contest sponsored by his employer Poe considered a professional breach.

Hewitt saw the matter differently. Though editor of the *Visiter*, he saw no conflict of interest. Since he was not being remunerated to edit the magazine, he felt free to enter a contest it sponsored. His entry did not seem unprofessional to him because Hewitt did not consider himself a professional. His actions were not unprecedented. *The Bouquet*, a Boston literary magazine that had sponsored a contest the previous year, told contestants, 'The editor has the privilege of becoming a competitor.'[3]

Poe's reaction demonstrates what intense emotions contests could unleash. Since writing was largely an amateur endeavour, a contest offered a rare way to compensate authors. The *Visiter* let winners choose between cash or prizes. Poe chose cash, receiving fifty dollars for his winning tale. Instead of the twenty-five-dollar poetry prize, Hewitt chose a silver cup. Losing this extra twenty-five dollars fuelled Poe's anger. He *was* robbed: 'The Coliseum' is far superior to Hewitt's poem.

The speaker of 'The Coliseum', a traveller wishing to immerse himself in Rome's heritage, seeks 'springs of lore' within the ancient ruins. After much weary travel, he takes strength in what the Coliseum represents. His words echo Fingal's contemplation of the ruins of Balclutha, a walled town belonging to the ancient Britons in 'Carthon', one of James Macpherson's Ossianic poems. Fingal intones, 'The thistle shook there its lonely head: the moss whistled to the wind.' Poe's traveller observes, 'Here, where the dames of Rome their gilded hair / Waved to the wind, now wave the reed and thistle!' (ll. 21–2). Shrugging off his melancholy, Poe's traveller listens to what the ruins say. The idea that building stone could retain memories of what has occurred within the Coliseum may seem fanciful, but Poe understood how sensitive, imaginative minds could unlock memories stored within physical objects.

Reprinting 'The Coliseum' two years later, Poe subtitled it 'A Prize Poem', thus awarding himself the recognition the contest judges had denied. Ten years later he still resented their decision, according to the biographical essay Henry Hirst contributed to the Philadelphia *Saturday Museum*. Though Hirst wrote the essay, Poe supplied much of its detail. Hirst said '*both* premiums were awarded' to Poe 'although, among the competitors were many of the most celebrated names in our literature'.[4]

In the late 1820s and early 1830s, publishers sponsored contests to gain notoriety for their magazines and to increase both subscriptions and advertising revenues. But many of them genuinely wished to encourage the development of American literature. Sometimes contests awarded prizes for different genres – essays, poems, tales – but premiums for fiction were typically the highest. In other words, contests assigned a commercial value to literature. Poe wanted most to be a poet, but contests made him realize that fiction was more lucrative. He changed focus and began writing short stories.

Poe relished a good competition. The *Visiter* contest was not his first. Two years earlier the Philadelphia *Saturday Courier* had offered a hundred-dollar premium for the best tale. News of this contest spread north to New Hampshire and south to the Carolinas.[5] Poe was living in Baltimore when he heard about it. With nowhere else to go after leaving West Point, he had returned to his Aunt Maria Clemm's Baltimore home in Mechanic's Row on Wilkes Street, Fells Point, where he shared cramped quarters with his ailing brother Henry, his adolescent cousin Virginia and their bedridden grandmother. Through sheer tenacity, Maria Clemm held the household together. Mayne Reid, who enjoyed her hospitality years later, characterized Mrs Clemm as 'a type of those grand American mothers – such as existed in the days when block-houses had to be defended, bullets run in red-hot saucepans, and guns loaded for sons and husbands to fire them.'[6]

William James Bennett, *Baltimore from Federal Hill*, 1831.

Maria Clemm's mother, Elizabeth Cairnes Poe, received a modest annuity after the death of her husband, Revolutionary patriot David Poe, Sr, which supplied the family's main source of income. Anxious to contribute to the household and eager to pursue his literary career, Poe prepared several tales for the *Courier* contest. The more tales, he reckoned, the better his chances. By the deadline, 1 December 1831, contestants had submitted more than eighty stories, which the editor generally found 'striking, interesting, and well-told fictions'.[7]

Though the premium the *Courier* offered seems quite generous and its publisher's desire to encourage American literature heartfelt, a contest gave publishers a significant side benefit: it supplied original content without requiring them to remunerate authors. Contest submissions typically became property of the magazine, which could do with them whatever its editor wished. A good contest gave weeklies copy they could use for many weeks to come. The *Courier* kept publishing contest entries through the following year, sometimes using them as lead articles.

Less than a month after the deadline, the judges had reached their decision. To Poe's chagrin, Delia S. Bacon won the contest for 'Love's Martyr', a tragic tale of a young woman betrothed to a British officer who ventures from her frontier village to see him but is slain accidentally by Indians sent to escort her. One South Carolina editor thought 'Love's Martyr' an excellent choice, finding it 'beautiful and interesting'.[8] Poe questioned the quality of Bacon's writing. She reused this episode for *The Bride of Fort Edward*, which Poe reviewed. 'Nothing less than a long apprenticeship to letters will give the author . . . even a chance to be remembered or considered', he observed. Her prose 'stands sadly in need of a straight jacket'.[9]

Under the heading 'Prize Tale', the *Courier* published 'Love's Martyr' on 7 January 1832. 'Metzengerstein', which appeared the week after, may have come in second. The differences between Bacon's tale and Poe's are obvious from the outset. 'Love's Martyr' begins: 'It was almost morning; the deep blue of the midnight heaven had half faded, and the stars were going out, one by one, in that pale dome, as though the glory they had all night showered upon the silent earth, had exhausted their eternal fountains of brightness.' Poe was right: her prose does need a straitjacket. Before this first sentence is over, her wordiness devolves into nonsense. If the fountains of brightness are eternal, how can they be exhausted?

'Metzengerstein', in contrast, begins with a brief yet elegant pronouncement: 'Horror and fatality have been stalking abroad in all ages.' This memorable opening emphasizes the indisputable existence of evil. The conjoined word pair that forms the sentence's subject identifies the tale's frightening nature. Personification lends humanlike qualities to horror and fatality while making them something other than human. Monsterlike, they are immortal creatures forever roaming the planet. Poe thus treats the eternal with subtlety, without using the word 'eternal'. Whereas Bacon's phrase, 'eternal fountains of brightness', embodies a cliché typically used to describe enduring goodness, Poe's sentence emphasizes the omnipresence of evil. Bacon depicts eternity as a manifestation of God's benevolence; Poe portrays man's contact with eternity as an encounter fraught with fear.[10]

The judges obviously read beyond the opening sentences to decide the winner. Bacon's subject matter may have played a part in their decision. A romantic story set in the past, 'Love's Martyr' belongs to the genre of historical romance, the most respected form of fiction among contemporary American readers, as the ongoing popularity of Sir Walter Scott and James Fenimore Cooper shows. Indeed, Bacon's plot closely resembles *The Last of the Mohicans*. Jingoistic critics believed American authors should take their inspiration from American subjects. Announcing a fiction contest in 1832, the publisher of the *Cincinnati Mirror* suggested competitors set their tales in the Ohio Valley or, at least, link their stories to regional history.[11] The literary contest could reinforce style as well as subject. Editors encouraged authors to write what readers wanted most: historical romance.

Gothic fiction, with its Old World settings, had been around since the late eighteenth century, but it was not regarded as highly as historical romance among nineteenth-century American readers, who considered it derivative of German literature. Critiques of Poe's Gothicism or 'Germanism' would dog him throughout his career. For a later reprinting of 'Metzengerstein' he added a subtitle – 'A Tale in Imitation of the German' – to forestall further criticism, making it an homage to the literary tradition. 'Metzengerstein' is a Gothic experiment, an effort that celebrates the Gothic and advances its possibilities.

The idea that American authors must use American themes and settings for their work was a parochial notion, Poe recognized. All they really needed to do was write well: they should feel free to use whatever themes and settings they wished. While Poe chose a Gothic setting for 'Metzengerstein' – the castles of eastern Europe

– he experimented with different modes of discourse, contrasting narrative strategies, multiple voices and innovative visual imagery. 'Metzengerstein' was a deliberately difficult work. Psychical researcher Theodore Besterman called it 'a farrago in which no precise meaning can be found'.[12] Poe's daring experiments testify to his confidence. A more conservative approach could have made a more likely contest winner.

In 'Letter to Mr —', written the same year as 'Metzengerstein', Poe outlined his groundbreaking poetic theory. He observed, 'A poem, in my opinion, is opposed to a work of science by having, for its *immediate* object, pleasure, not truth.'[13] When Poe switched from poetry to tales, he applied his poetic principles to fiction. Besides maximizing the delightful aspects of literature and minimizing its instructive purpose, he sought to give each work a 'unity of effect'. 'Metzengerstein' embodies such unity.[14] Never before had anyone approached fiction with the consummate level of artistry Poe brought to it. Never before had anyone suggested a tale need have no other purpose than to delight. Abandoning the delight-and-instruct paradigm, Poe created a new aesthetic and paved the way for modern fiction.

'Metzengerstein' is also daring in its details. For example, the mysterious, witch-like old crone was a staple of Gothic fiction, but Poe gave this traditional motif new life. After introducing the Berlifitzings and the Metzengersteins – two feuding Hungarian families – the narrator illustrates their differences: 'It was remarked by an old crone of haggard, and sinister appearance, that fire and water might sooner mingle, than a Berlifitzing clasp the hand of a Metzengerstein.'[15] These words reinforce the tale's innovativeness. This early in the story, even before the narrator has fully established his narrative control, he temporarily relinquishes it to give voice to an evil woman.

The old woman's image contributes to the tale's visual complexity as well, creating the effect of a cinematic cutaway shot.

Poe's imagery frequently anticipates a visual aesthetic that would not emerge until the invention of motion pictures – mainly because his writing profoundly influenced cinema's development. Poe's short fiction gave pioneering filmmakers a structural model. One early screenwriting manual recommends reading 'The Fall of the House of Usher' to understand how to combine setting and action into a unified whole.[16] Sergei Eisenstein said that 'The Sphinx', in which Poe juxtaposes a nearby insect with a faraway landscape to make it resemble a distant monster, greatly influenced his foreground composition.[17]

'Metzengerstein' relates the rivalry between the last surviving members of both families, Wilhelm, Count Berlifitzing, and Frederick, Baron Metzengerstein. Berlifitzing, a doting old man, spends his time with his horses. The teenaged Metzengerstein lives a life of debauchery, lavishly indulging his passions and his cruelties. One night at the young baron's instigation the count's stables catch fire. Berlifitzing perishes in the blaze, from which emerges a demonic horse – his soul reincarnated in equine form.

Baron Metzengerstein's attachment to the horse seems perverse. Neighbours cannot understand why he spends so much time

Jane Fonda as Comtesse Fréderique Metzengerstein in Roger Vadim's 'Metzengerstein', the first segment of the omnibus film *Histoires extraordinaires* (1968).

riding the animal. But the baron does not choose to ride the horse. Rather, this supernatural beast compels him to ride. As Metzengerstein shrieks his final shriek, the scene switches from long shot to extreme close up: 'The agony of his countenance, the convulsive struggling of his frame gave evidence of superhuman exertion; but no sound, save a solitary shriek, escaped from his lacerated lips, which were bitten through and through, in the intensity of terror.'[18] The vivid imagery, the tension-filled terror, the exciting conclusion: 'Metzengerstein' hardly reads like a young author's first published tale. It is the work of a master storyteller.

Poe's other entries to the *Courier* contest include 'The Bargain Lost', a parody of Gothic fiction patterned on the Faust legend; 'A Decided Loss', which spoofs the extravagant fiction in *Blackwood's Edinburgh Magazine*; 'The Duke de L'Omelette', a story of a supercilious French duke who dies in disgust at the sight of an improperly prepared ortolan and ends up playing cards with the Devil; and 'A Tale of Jerusalem', a humorous historical tale inspired by the erudite English novelist Horace Smith and involving a prank ancient Romans play on Jews defending Jerusalem.

Like 'Metzengerstein', these tales show their author experimenting with new techniques in terms of style, subject and narrative strategy. 'A Decided Loss' is the earliest known story Poe wrote in first person. Overall, his sophisticated manipulation of the first-person narrative may be his most important contribution to the history of fiction. This early in his career, he was already experimenting with the form. 'A Decided Loss' is a tale told by a dead man, a narrative strategy that would not achieve acceptance until the twentieth century.[19]

'The Bargain Lost' makes fun of the weighty descriptive passages from Gothic novels. 'I hold minute attention to trifles unworthy the dignity of serious narrative', the narrator says. 'Otherwise I might here, following the example of the novelist, dilate on the subject of habiliment, and other mere matters of the outward man.'[20] The narrator then presents an absurdly detailed account of what he might have said. To suit his satirical purpose, Poe mimicked the Gothic style, using the biggest novelistic cliché of all time: 'It was a dark and stormy night.' 'The Bargain Lost' also shows Poe developing his fine sense of humour. Speaking with Pedro Garcia, a Venetian metaphysician, the Devil surveys the culinary value of the souls he has eaten. The soul of the comic playwright Terence, for example, was 'firm as an Esquimaux, and juicy as a German'.[21] Imbibing copious amounts of Sauterne, Pedro loses his inhibitions and offers the Devil his soul, suggesting he cook it in a stew or, perhaps, a ragout. A discriminating gourmand, the Devil is incensed by Pedro's culinary suggestions and indignantly lets him keep his soul.

Representing different literary styles while simultaneously burlesquing them, Poe's early tales demonstrate his command of contemporary fiction. He may be best known as a Gothic writer, but the stylistic virtuosity of his early fiction shows he did not want to be identified with any particular literary movement. Once he made up his mind to write short stories, he embraced nearly every form of prose fiction and invented original modes of discourse, new narrative approaches, and different ways of telling tales no one had used previously. Edgar Allan Poe is the greatest innovator in American literature.

There was another reason why he took so many different approaches in his early tales: he conceived them as part of a unified story cycle, which he planned to call *Tales of the Folio Club*. Though the *Courier* contest provided the impetus for him to shift from poet to storyteller, he was dissatisfied with leaving his tales as fugitive pieces, that is, separately published articles. The Folio Club framework let him intersperse tales with burlesque criticism, which would bind the collection together, enhancing his parody of contemporary fiction and spoofing current trends in literary criticism.

A. G. Learned, *Mrs Maria Poe Clemm*, 1916.

Through 1831 he continued living with Maria Clemm. Edgar and his brother Henry shared the attic. Henry, who also shared an interest in poetry, was failing fast, a victim of consumption and dissipation. Whatever late night literary conversation the Poe brothers had was punctuated by the sound of Henry's blood-and-sputum cough, a cough that sounded like a death rattle. Henry Poe died on 1 August 1831. Poe would pay homage to his brother in *The Narrative of Arthur Gordon Pym*, having Augustus, the title character's best friend, die the same day.

That same year Poe fell in love with Mary Starr, a pretty teen-aged girl with auburn hair who lived just around the corner from the Clemms. Mary's recollection of 'Eddie', though double-filtered through the passage of fifty years and the creative reshaping of a kinsman, rings true. Her physical description of him is precise. 'About five feet eight inches tall', he had 'dark, almost black hair, which he wore long and brushed back in student style over his ears. It was as fine as silk. His eyes were large and full, gray and piercing.' He was 'entirely clean-shaven. His nose was long and straight, and his features finely cut. The expression about his mouth was beautiful. He was pale, and had no colour. His skin was of clear, beautiful olive.'[22]

Mary and Eddie started seeing each other almost daily. Poe admired the poetry of Robert Burns, which he quoted often. Poe made Burns's Mary suit his own:

We hae plighted our troth, my Mary,
In mutual affection to join,
And curst be the cause that shall part us!
The hour, and the moment o' time!

Occasionally Mary and Eddie would spend their evenings seated on the stoop of her uncle's home. At other times they would go out walking beyond the city limits to the surrounding hills. As their relationship grew serious, her family warned Mary away from this poet without prospects.

On his part Poe began feeling as if the two had plighted their troth. Like anyone with ambition, he had a jealous streak. One time, when Mary played their song – Thomas Moore's 'Come Rest in This Bosom' – for someone else, he flew into a rage, snatching the music from the piano and dashing it to the floor: an early indication of his mercurial temper. A quarrel ensued, but Mary and Eddie later patched up their differences.

One evening when they planned to meet, Eddie did not show. Mary waited at the parlour window until ten o'clock. When Mrs Starr saw her daughter crying, she told her to go upstairs to bed. Mary hesitated to abandon her vigil.

Poe soon showed up at her window. He was drunk. She had known him for months now, but this was the first time she had seen him after a cup too much. One time was enough. This incident proved the cause that would part them. Poe had an extremely low tolerance for alcohol. His habit of drinking on an empty stomach exacerbated the problem. A single glass of champagne, Mayne Reid observed, affected him so much 'that he was hardly any longer responsible for his actions'.[23] Just a few drinks gave him an insatiable craving for more. At Poe's insistence, Mary came outside and sat on the stoop with him.

As they talked, Poe either said something or did something that spooked her. She jumped off the stoop, ran through the alleyway to the back of their house, and rushed inside to her mother.

'Mary! Mary!' Mrs Starr exclaimed. 'What's the matter?'

Before her daughter could answer, Poe entered the room. Mrs Starr told Mary to go upstairs to her room. She went.

'I want to talk to your daughter,' Poe said. 'If you don't tell her to come downstairs, I will go after her. I have a right to.'

'You have no right to,' Mrs Starr told him as she blocked the way upstairs. 'You cannot go upstairs.'

'I have a right,' Poe insisted. 'She is my wife now in the sight of Heaven.'

Mrs Starr told him he had better go home and go to bed. He went.

Since Mary's recollection forms the only source for this episode, Poe's side of the story has gone unrecorded. Based on similar episodes, his reaction is not hard to fathom. Severe hangovers confined him to bed for days. Once a hangover subsided, deep remorse and profound self-loathing persisted. He made several attempts to contact Mary, but her family prevented him from seeing her.

Living in Baltimore, Poe found some local hangouts to his liking, including the bookstores. According to tradition, Edward J. Coale's, located on Calvert just north of Baltimore Street, was one bookshop that lured Poe within its doors. Amiable, easy-going and warm-hearted, Coale was just the kind of man willing to extend his hospitality to a down-and-out poet.[24] Widow Meagher's place, an oyster stand and liquor bar located on Pratt and Calvert, was reputedly another Poe hangout. The regulars at Widow Meagher's nicknamed Poe 'Bard'. 'Bard, come up and take a nip,' they would say. Or, 'Bard, take a hand in this game.'

Living up to his nickname, Poe would compose impromptu verses at Widow Meagher's request. According to an anonymous acquaintance, 'Poe always complied, writing many a witty couplet and at times poems of considerable length. Much of his poetical work, quite as meritorious as some by which his name was immortalized, was thus frittered into obscurity.'[25]

Of all the people Poe met in Baltimore, none became a greater friend than Lambert Wilmer. 'Almost every day we took long walks in the rural districts near Baltimore,' Wilmer remembered, 'and had long conversations on a great variety of subjects.' Their talk often turned to literature. Poe was critical of many authors, Wilmer recalled, but he admired the poetry of Alfred Tennyson and enjoyed the prose of Benjamin Disraeli.[26]

Poe shared the manuscript of *Tales of the Folio Club* with Wilmer in the summer of 1832. Honoured by the gesture, Wilmer conveyed his appreciation of Poe's tales in the *Visiter*. Writing in the editorial plural, Wilmer reported: 'We have read these tales, every syllable, with the greatest pleasure, and for originality, richness of imagery, and purity of the style, few American authors in our opinion have produced any thing superior.'[27] Wilmer hoped to publish some in the *Visiter* but never got the chance. It was around this time that Cloud dismissed him. Soured by the experience, Wilmer left Baltimore before year's end.

After his departure, Poe attempted to work with Hewitt, submitting some verses for possible publication in the *Visiter* in 1833. Hewitt accepted them. 'Enigma' appeared in the third week of April. This clever sixteen-line puzzle poem challenges the reader's literary knowledge. For example, the eleventh line – 'The bard that paints imagination's powers' – stands for Mark Akenside, the author of *Pleasures of the Imagination*. Readers who guess all the poetic names correctly can solve the poem's last two lines: 'These names when rightly read, a name [make] known / Which gathers all their glories in its own.' The answer, of course, is Shakespeare.

Other poems Poe published in the *Visiter* in 1833 include 'Serenade', 'To —', and 'Fanny'. All are slight works. He withheld his best material from the magazine after Hewitt became editor. Poe had bigger plans for his fiction. In the first week of May he approached the *New England Magazine*, proposing to publish *Tales of the Folio Club* serially. Founded in 1831 by Edwin Buckingham with the help of his father, Joseph Buckingham, the magazine embodied Edwin's youthful literary enthusiasm. It gained a nationwide reputation, earning respect from readers, who enjoyed its high quality, and from authors, who appreciated being paid a tidy one dollar per page.[28] Poe asked the Buckinghams to publish his complete story cycle, now called *Eleven Tales of the Arabesque*. As a sample, he sent 'Epimanes'.[29]

The story features Antiochus Epiphanes, the ancient Syrian monarch known as Epimanes (Madman), whom Poe knew from reading Polybius. Poe took great liberties with his source, having Epimanes parade through the streets of Antioch in an outlandish giraffe suit. Appalled at the sight, the city's lions and tigers and leopards, all domesticated and working as valets, rise up against the king. The plot is silly, but 'Epimanes' remains notable for its experiments in narrative form. The narrator speaks to his readers like a tour guide leading them through the past, and stand-ins for

John H. B.
Latrobe, *c.* 1875.

the reader ask questions. 'Epimanes' thus challenges traditional
barriers between narrator and reader.

In practical terms, the story was the victim of bad timing. The
same month Poe sent 'Epimanes' to the *New England Magazine*,
Edwin Buckingham died at sea. Joseph Buckingham assumed sole
editorship, but his heart was not in it. Poe never received a response.
Instead he submitted *Tales of the Folio Club* to the *Visiter* contest.

In the first week of October 1833 the contest judges – John H. B.
Latrobe, John Pendleton Kennedy, Dr James H. Miller – decided

the winners. The three gathered at Latrobe's home with a sufficient supply of fine wine and good cigars to see them through. Poe had submitted his tales in a bound notebook, which they saved until last. Intrigued, Latrobe read the volume straight through, interrupted occasionally by Kennedy and Miller.

'Capital!' one would exclaim. Or, 'Excellent!' Or, perhaps, 'How odd!'

They found much evidence of genius. 'There was no uncertain grammar,' Latrobe recalled, 'no feeble phraseology, no ill-placed punctuation, no worn-out truism, no strong thought elaborated into weakness.'[30] The only hard part was deciding which tale to choose as the winner, but they ultimately selected 'Manuscript Found in a Bottle'.

The *Visiter* contest brought Poe in contact with its judges. Listening to him talk about his writings, Latrobe became entranced. Poe 'seemed to forget the world around him, as wild fancy, logical truth, mathematical analysis, and wonderful combinations of fact flowed, in strange commingling, from his lips, in words choice and appropriate as though the result of the closest study'.[31] When Latrobe asked what else he was writing, Poe said 'he was engaged in a voyage to the moon, and at once went into a somewhat learned disquisition upon the laws of gravity, the height of the earth's atmosphere, and the capacities of balloons, warming in his speech as he proceeded'.[32] What Latrobe heard was the beginnings of 'Hans Pfaall', a long story about a balloon voyage into outer space. Previous works of science fiction had been heavily didactic, utopian tales. Poe was the first to remove science fiction from the realm of the didactic and celebrate it for its own sake. As Jorge Luis Borges observed, 'What today is called science-fiction originated with Poe.'[33]

Kennedy, a popular novelist, encouraged him to publish *Tales of the Folio Club*. Poe entrusted the manuscript to Kennedy who sent it to Philadelphia publisher Henry Carey in November. For the next several months, Poe eagerly expected news from Philadelphia concerning the fate of his manuscript. At the end of March 1834, he received some unexpected news from Virginia.

John Allan, his foster father, was dead.

2

The Birth of a Poet

America lured people from Scotland to its shores throughout the eighteenth century. In the final decade an ambitious, teenaged youth named John Allan left Irvine, an Ayrshire seaport, for Richmond, Virginia, where he worked for his uncle William Galt, a wealthy merchant. With business partner Charles Ellis, Allan established a mercantile firm in 1800. Three years later he married Frances Valentine. Mr and Mrs Allan soon realized they could not have children. Or, to be precise, they discovered Mrs Allan could not have children: Mr Allan's philandering proved him quite capable of fatherhood. The Allans shared an interest in the stage, often attending the Richmond Theatre on Broad Street. When it opened its doors for a new season in August 1811, the theatre featured one of the nation's most beautiful and talented actresses: Elizabeth Poe.

Born into a family of English actors, Elizabeth Arnold had come to America as a child with her actress mother. She performed on the American stage in her adolescence, establishing a solid reputation. Elizabeth married young; her first husband died before she was out of her teens. She wed her second husband, David Poe, Jr, in April 1806. He became an actor – still a disreputable, poorly paid profession – without his family's approval. His acting talents in no way approached hers, but the two patched together a precarious living. She took little time off despite giving birth to three children over the next four years. William Henry Leonard Poe, known as Henry, was born 30 January 1807. Edgar was born in Boston on

Elizabeth Arnold Hopkins Poe, 1914.

19 January 1809. And their sister Rosalie was born 20 December 1810. The family travelled the eastern seaboard as the young parents performed in the major cities. In July 1811 they were living in Norfolk, Virginia, where David deserted Elizabeth and the children after a vicious quarrel.[1]

Elizabeth, now desperate, welcomed an invitation from the manager of the Richmond Theatre in August. Though suffering from tuberculosis, she was anxious to use her talents to help the children. She performed through September. By mid-October, her health had worsened. Unable to perform, she lost her sole means of support. Her plight touched the heartstrings of Richmond's theatregoers. Celebrity misfortune holds a macabre allure. Strangers visited to gawk at Elizabeth, to see the pitiful sight of the lovely actress in her sickbed with her starving children nearby. A local merchant wryly observed that this season Mrs Poe's sick chamber was 'the most fashionable place of resort'.[2]

Frances Allan and her friend Jane Mackenzie visited the ailing actress. They were moved by the sight of her children. Elizabeth Poe died on 8 December 1811. Her husband's whereabouts remained unknown, but he apparently succumbed to tuberculosis himself and died soon afterwards. Henry went to Baltimore to live with his grandparents. Jane Mackenzie adopted Rosalie. Frances Allan convinced her husband to take the younger boy into their family. Sometimes they called him Edgar Allan, but he remained a foster child. Mrs Allan adored him. Mr Allan tolerated the boy to please his wife.

Ellis and Allan became profitable enough in the coming years that the partners decided to open a London branch. In 1815 John and Frances Allan left Richmond for London, taking with them Edgar, now six, and Frances's unmarried sister Ann Valentine – Aunt Nancy. They disembarked at Liverpool and travelled north to Scotland, where they visited friends and members of the Allan clan.

John Allan has gone down in history as mean-spirited, tough-minded and cold-hearted, but he seldom behaved wickedly toward his foster son. His British correspondence is sometimes quite sweet. Informing Ellis they had arrived safely, Allan wrote while his foster son looked on.[3]

'Pa,' said Edgar. 'Say something for me, say I was not afraid coming across the Sea.'

Edgar's words exhibit characteristic behaviour. He wanted others to know he had successfully faced a challenge. After their Scottish sojourn, they reached London in the first week of October 1815. By month's end, they found lodgings in Bloomsbury at 47 Southampton Row, Russell Square, near the British Museum. Later they would relocate to 39 Southampton Row, which Poe would make the setting for 'Why the Little Frenchman Wears His Hand in a Sling'.

In April 1816 Poe entered the London boarding school of the Misses Dubourg, where he learned English grammar and composition. Selections from Joseph Addison and Oliver Goldsmith provided models for composition. Selections from John Milton and James Thomson offered models for verse – models against which Poe would rebel. From the Dubourgs, he acquired a copy of the *Book of Common Prayer*. Intended to indoctrinate him in the fundamentals of the Anglican Church, the *Book of Common Prayer* gave him another model of English prose, one perhaps more attractive than the selections in his composition textbook. His other readings came largely from the Augustan Age, but the prose of the Anglican prayer book, with its formal diction and long periods, recalled the Elizabethan.[4]

Poe left the Dubourgs in late 1817 or early 1818 to attend the Manor House School, Stoke Newington, then about four miles from London. The school and its overseer, the Reverend John Bransby, would receive fictional treatment in 'William Wilson'. Poe charac- terized the place as 'a misty-looking village' filled with 'gigantic and gnarled trees' and houses 'excessively ancient and inordinately tall'.[5] Giving students a grounding in the classics, Bransby also taught English literature and history, frequently tossing off apt quotations from Shakespeare.[6]

The London branch proved unsuccessful. John Allan closed the office in 1820 and brought his family back to Richmond. Ellis found the Allans 'a little Englishised' upon their return but predicted that their Englishness would soon wear off.[7] Allan enrolled Edgar in a classical school run by Joseph H. Clarke, a hot-tempered, pedantic, Irish bachelor from Trinity College, Dublin. 'Only the pure Latinity of the Augustan age', Clarke would tell parents repeatedly to assure them of the quality of education he provided.[8]

Students sharpened their Latin by capping verses or, for a greater challenge, double-capping them, a competition at which Poe excelled. Besides reading much Latin poetry and history at Clarke's school, Poe began studying Greek. Since his teacher believed in a well-rounded education, Poe also learned maths and science during his three years with Clarke. He excelled in elocution as well. One year he competed in a city-wide elocution contest and took home the prize. He wrote poetry while Clarke's student, hoping to publish a collection of his schoolboy verse, an early indication of his literary ambition.[9]

Poe's athleticism complemented his intellect. Schoolmate John Preston called him 'a swift runner, a wonderful leaper, and what was more rare, a boxer'. Thomas Ellis, the son of Allan's business partner, became his protégé. Poe taught him how to shoot, swim and play field hockey. Preston remembered a footrace between Clarke's and another school. Fellow students chose Poe to represent them. 'The race came off one bright May morning at sunrise, on the Capitol Square', Preston remembered. 'Poe ran well; but his competitor was a long-legged, Indian-looking fellow, who would have outstripped Atalanta without the help of the golden apple.'[10] Atalanta? Preston was recalling an episode from Ovid. It seems Poe was not the only student to leave Clarke's school with a working knowledge of the classics.

Poe's most renowned athletic feat was a six-mile swim down the James River – which he undertook on a wager. Several friends accompanied him in a boat. As his back grew sunburned, they urged him to quit. He refused. Upon accepting a challenge, Poe would not back down. By the time he finished, he had first- and second-degree burns on his back and neck. He resembled a boiled lobster, one eyewitness said, but he successfully completed the swim.[11]

Regardless of his intellectual and athletic prowess, Poe did not always receive his classmates' respect. Those who considered themselves part of Richmond aristocracy looked down on him. Preston explained, 'Of Edgar Poe it was known that his parents were players, and that he was dependent upon the bounty that is bestowed upon an adopted son.'[12] Poe's insecurity about his upbringing, combined with his romantic inclinations, prompted him to invent elaborate fictions about his early life.

When Clarke left Richmond in 1823, Poe transferred to William Burke's academy, another excellent local school. John Allan took pains to give his foster child the education of a proper gentleman. Since Poe's classical knowledge outstripped that of his fellow students, he pursued independent study. One classmate at Burke's remembered him finishing assignments quickly and devoting time to desultory reading and creative writing.[13]

Poe left Burke's in March 1825, the month William Galt died. A lifelong bachelor, Galt bequeathed a considerable portion of his estate to John Allan. By one estimate Allan inherited three-quarters of a million dollars. He soon purchased Moldavia, a grand brick home in Richmond at the corner of Main and Fifth. Across the street lived the Royster family. When Edgar, now sixteen, caught sight of their teenaged daughter Elmira, he fell in love.

Elmira found him 'beautiful' but 'not very talkative'.[14] In short, she too fell in love. Before he went to university, they considered themselves engaged. Disliking their relationship, her father did what he could to separate them. He intercepted Edgar's letters to Elmira and prevented her from writing him. Each assumed the other had lost interest, and their relationship cooled. Her father ultimately arranged her marriage to local businessman Alexander Shelton.

Poe reached the University of Virginia in February 1826. Just one year old, it was already among the finest institutions of higher learning in the nation – largely due to the Herculean efforts of its founder Thomas Jefferson, who designed the campus, hired the faculty, planned the curriculum, established the library and served as rector. One progressive aspect of Jefferson's curriculum concerned the amount of personal choice students had to create their own plan of study. They could take whichever courses they wished.

According to Poe, Allan prevented him from taking full advantage of the innovative curriculum. Most students took three courses, but Allan, despite his newfound wealth, had not provided Poe with sufficient funds to afford tuition for a third class. In addition to

Ancient Languages and Modern Languages, Poe had intended
to take Mathematics. Neither had Allan provided basic college
expenses. Poe had to borrow money locally at usurious rates to
buy textbooks. One book he acquired in college was *The Satires
of Persius* in Sir William Drummond's English/Latin parallel text
edition. His copy, which survives at the University of Virginia, is
inscribed with his name and dated '1826, Virginia College'. The
work's influence on Poe has so far gone unnoticed, but Persius's
satire of literary trends in ancient Rome provided another inspiration for Poe's satirical poetry and fiction.

Professor George Blaetterman taught Modern Languages:
French, Italian and Spanish. Though, a 'rather a rough looking
German', he possessed, as Jefferson said, an 'excellent mind and
high qualifications'.[15] One week Blaetterman challenged Poe's class
to translate a passage from Tasso into English verse. Poe accepted
the challenge – the only student who did – and Blaetterman
subsequently 'paid a very high compliment to his performance'.[16]
Professor George Long came from Cambridge University. Jefferson
had wanted someone to teach Greek, Latin, and Hebrew but
realized the only way to get a Hebrew scholar would be to hire
a clergyman, which he adamantly refused. Long taught Latin
and Greek, supplementing his linguistic courses with lessons
in ancient geography.

Outside the classroom Poe had other opportunities to pursue his
passion for literature. He joined the Jefferson Society and became

Detail from *A Bright Spot* [A Panoramic View of the University of Virginia], 1911.

its secretary. Members discussed what books they read, made recommendations for reading and shared writings of their own composition. On one occasion, Poe read a tale he had written only to have his friends laugh at it. Incensed, he flung the manuscript into the fire. Classmate Thomas Goode Tucker also remembered Poe 'quoting authors and reading poetic productions of his own' and reading the histories of David Hume and John Lingard.[17]

Tucker's reminiscence reveals an important moment in Poe's university experience, one requiring some elaboration. Jefferson dreaded that students might learn English history solely by reading David Hume's *History of England*. He ordered books for the university library refuting Hume – George Brodie's *History of the British Empire*, John Lingard's *History of England* – and personally recommended them to students.[18] Henry Tutwiler, one student who dined at Monticello, vividly remembered Jefferson's attitude: 'He used to say that the reading of Hume would make an English Tory, and that the transition to an American Tory was an easy one. He never failed to recommend to the youthful student, as an antidote to Hume, Brodie's *British Empire*; the latter, he said, had "pulverized" Hume.'[19] Though Jefferson often invited students to Sunday dinner at Monticello, there is no direct evidence that Poe dined with him. According to Tutwiler, Jefferson's dinner invitations were both systematic and insistent. If a student were unable to visit Monticello when invited, Jefferson invited him again. During these dinners, he talked books with students and advised them what to read. The conclusion is obvious: Poe may have read Hume on his own, but he read Lingard on Jefferson's advice.

Poe's literary interests took him from the dining room at Monticello to the back room of a Charlottesville second-hand store, where clerk Peter Pease was buying a copy of William Hogarth's *Works* in instalments. Poe invited Pease to his dorm room, an increasingly renowned place for intimate, late night intellectual conversation. As they examined Hogarth's engravings, Poe suggested they gamble for it. A throw of the dice would settle the matter. Whoever won would get the book; whoever lost would pay for it. Poe lost.[20]

Final exams were scheduled for December. Poe wrote to Allan complaining how unfair it was that junior students like him would be examined with the seniors.[21] Poe's letter was just a ploy for sympathy. Juniors and seniors were examined separately. Poe *chose* to be examined with the seniors – and did quite well. He placed among the top students in both the senior Latin class and the senior French class.[22] Why did Poe choose to be tested with the seniors? His competitive spirit partly explains his choice. He always had a desire to prove himself, to lift himself above the level of his peers. His financial difficulties gave him a practical reason for advancing quickly. If Allan would only pay for two courses per term, so be it. Poe would advance through his classes in half the time, giving himself the opportunity to take courses in different subjects in his second year at school.

This was not to be the case. Poe had compensated for Allan's stinginess by gambling recklessly. He incurred huge gambling debts – around two thousand dollars, according to contemporary estimates. With a good memory, an ability to imagine what others were thinking and excellent mathematical skills, Poe had the makings of a good gambler, but one crucial aspect of his personality prevented him from gambling success: he could not back down from a challenge. Hearing the phrase, 'Double or nothing', or words to that effect, Poe could not resist. Allan refused to honour his debts and withdrew him from university in December.

Embittered by Allan's neglect, Poe returned to Richmond and moved back into Moldavia. Allan put him to work in the counting room at Ellis and Allan, where Poe could learn accounting, book-keeping and commercial correspondence.[23] To an aspiring poet, few endeavours could be more distasteful. The two quarrelled frequently. By mid-March Poe had moved out. He remained in Richmond briefly but took passage to Boston without saying goodbye. Allan assumed he had gone to sea.

Boston seems an odd destination for Poe. Philadelphia, which rivalled New York as the nation's most important literary centre, would seem more amenable. But Poe had his reasons for choosing Boston. Of all the major American cities, it was the furthest from Richmond, and he wanted to distance himself from John Allan. Besides, Boston was his birthplace. Returning there offered him a way to be reborn, to start afresh, to make himself into the person he wanted to be. And Poe wanted most to be a poet.

He reached Boston at the end of March 1827, carrying with him a sheaf of manuscript verse. He needed a job but spent time tinker-ing with his poems, making last-minute revisions, getting them ready to publish. Within the next month or two he met Calvin F. S. Thomas, a young printer eager to expand his business. Many have wondered why Thomas risked publishing a collection of verse from this unknown eighteen-year-old poet. But when Poe got to talking about his work, his enthusiasm was infectious. Thomas apparently became enthralled and agreed to issue the slender volume.

While the book was in press, Poe worked a variety of jobs, according to Peter Pease, who had also left Virginia for Boston. Seeing Poe one day, Pease hailed him. Surprised to hear his own name spoken aloud, Poe quickly approached, silencing Pease. They ducked into an alley, where Poe explained his odd behaviour. He implored Pease to keep his identity secret, explaining that 'he had left home to seek his fortune, and until he had hit it hard he preferred to remain incognito'. Poe said he had clerked in a wholesale merchant house, unsuccessfully sought editorial work and briefly worked on an obscure newspaper as a market reporter.[24]

Tamerlane and Other Poems, as Poe titled his first published book, preserved his anonymity but did not prevent him from later claiming its authorship. If the book proved successful, he could throw off the mantle of anonymity. For the time being, he identified himself on the title page solely as 'A Bostonian'. Though Poe would express condescension toward the Boston literary establishment in the coming years, this pseudonym verifies his desire to remake himself and suggests his early identification with his birthplace.

Barely forty pages long, *Tamerlane and Other Poems* consists of one long poem and several short ones. In 'Tamerlane', the thoroughly Byronic poem that opens the volume, the title character relates how he recognized his genius for leadership but fell in love, leaving his lover in order to pursue conquest but intending to return to make her queen. After conquering much of the world, he came back to find her dead. The price he paid for his kingdom was a broken heart. Reduced to plot summary 'Tamerlane' seems hackneyed. What makes it memorable is the nostalgia for lost youth Tamerlane articulates:

> 'Tis thus when the lovely summer sun
> Of our boyhood, his course hath run:
> For all we live to know – is known;
> And all we seek to keep – hath flown (ll. 384–7)

In childhood our imaginations are alive. As adults we enter the rational world. We gain knowledge yet lose our sense of wonder. This clash between the rational and the imaginative would pervade Poe's writings.

'The Lake' forms a fitting conclusion to the volume. Similarly nostalgic, its speaker recalls a lake he used to visit in his youth. After describing how it looked in daylight, he explains how its appearance changed at night. The night would throw a pall over the lake:

And the wind would pass me by
In its stilly melody,
My infant spirit would awake
To the terror of the lone lake. (ll. 9–12)

The speaker attempts to define the terror he had experienced. It was not fright, he asserts, 'But a tremulous delight, / And a feeling undefin'd, / Springing from a darken'd mind' (ll. 14–16). He can take delight in such terror because of his 'darken'd mind', a phrase indicating the speaker's lack of knowledge and experience. Poe borrowed the phrase from Byron's 'Stanzas'. 'The Lake' shifts its point of view from first to third person toward the end. Provocatively, the speaker's youthful self becomes someone else, someone 'Whose wild'ring thought could even make / An Eden of that dim lake' (ll. 20–21).

After arranging the publication of *Tamerlane and Other Poems*, Poe, now desperate, enlisted in the US Army on 26 May 1827. He was assigned to Battery H of the First Artillery in Fort Independence, Boston Harbor. His enlistment provided another reason for keeping his identity secret. John Allan had raised his foster son as a gentleman: the enlisted service consisted almost exclusively of the lower class.[25] Poe enlisted as Edgar A. Perry, a pseudonym reflecting his desire for military glory. He named himself after Commodore Oliver Hazard Perry, who bravely defeated the British in the Battle of Lake Erie and turned the tide of the War of 1812. Reporting the victory, Perry uttered his famous words: 'We have met the enemy and they are ours.' Vivid expressions of triumph always appealed to Poe.

A. Vizitelly, *Fort Moultrie, Charleston Harbor*, 1861.

Artillery work was gruelling and tedious. Poe was not averse to hard work, but his superiors recognized his education and abilities and in July appointed him clerk, a position which brought him close to the officers. From Boston Poe went to Fort Moultrie, off the coast of Charleston, South Carolina, arriving in mid-November. On 1 May 1828 he was promoted to artificer, a highly skilled position which put him in charge of making bombs at the fort. The position involved meticulous precision, much mathematical ability and considerable danger. Artificers calculated distance and trajectory and prepared gunpowder charges to suit.[26]

Initially, the army offered an outlet for Poe's ambition. Once he was promoted to sergeant major, the highest enlisted rank, on 1 January 1829, he grew restless. The term of his enlistment – five years – now seemed interminable. He sought his foster father's help. Allan coldly suggested he stay in the army for the entire enlistment. Poe took the suggestion as a challenge. How could he prove himself to Allan yet fulfil his ambition? Poe's solution was ingenious: he could attend the us Military Academy at West Point.

That way, he could get out of his enlistment while showing Allan that he was not a quitter. He would be escaping his enlistment not to stifle but to advance his military career. An appointment to the Academy offered him many advantages. He would receive the college education Allan had denied him at university. As an officer, Poe would have a much greater opportunity for military glory. He also foresaw himself in retirement. Still assuming he would be heir to Allan's fortune, Poe imagined himself as a paragon of Southern gentility, the kind of man who goes by 'Colonel' the rest of his life, writes poetry, ages gracefully and enjoys the finer things wealth can bring.

Charles Balthazar Julien Fevret de Saint-Mémin, *William Wirt*, 1807/8.

Amenable to Poe's new plan, Allan helped extricate him from his enlistment and arranged letters of recommendation. Officially discharged on 15 April 1829, Poe moved to Baltimore, where he assembled a new collection of poetry featuring 'Al Aaraaf', his longest and most challenging poem. In 'Al Aaraaf', Poe imagined an ideal world inhabited by angels and enlightened human souls who mediate between Heaven and the rest of the universe, conveying an awareness of beauty to the others and thus bringing them closer to God. To improve the poem, Poe sought the advice of William Wirt, Baltimore's grand old man of letters. Happy to help, Wirt nevertheless had trouble making sense of 'Al Aaraaf'. Diplomatically, he told Poe that he had not kept abreast of current literary trends.

To adorn *Al Aaraaf, Tamerlane and Minor Poems,* Poe included a number of literary quotations. The initial epigraph reads:

Entendes, Fabio, lo que voi deciendo?
Toma, si, lo entendio: – Mientes, Fabio.

Do you understand what I am saying to you, Fabio?
Yes, Thomas, I understand it. – You lie, Fabio.

Poe's source has escaped his editors, but these lines come from a sonnet by Lope de Vega he found in a magazine article by Manuel Eduardo de Gorostiza, which also quoted the next line: 'Que yo soi quien lo digo, y no lo entiendo' (For even I, who am telling it to you, do not understand it myself).[27] Anyone familiar with the sonnet could remember the line and recognize Poe's self-reflexive joke about the comprehensibility of 'Al Aaraaf'.

'Sonnet: To Science', as yet untitled, forms a verse preface to 'Al Aaraaf'. 'Tamerlane' follows 'Al Aaraaf', and the minor poems, some new, others revised from the earlier volume, come last. 'The Lake – to – ', for example, is a revised version of 'The Lake'. Poe's revisions show his increasing mastery of language and his shift toward vivid, concrete imagery. In the earlier version, the wind passes by 'in its stilly melody'. Poe deleted 'stilly' in revision to minimize his poetic language but also to eliminate a contradiction: how can the sound of the passing wind be characterized by stillness? Poe's revisions enhance the visual and aural imagery. The wind now looks and sounds more sinister, more foreboding: 'the black wind murmur'd by / In a dirge of melody' (ll. 9–10).

The feeling he described earlier as 'undefin'd, / Springing from a darken'd mind' he made more specific. Now it is a 'feeling not the jewell'd mine / Should ever bribe me to define / Nor Love – altho' the Love be thine' (ll. 15–17). Besides eliminating an obvious Byronism, he also emphasized the importance of the irrational delight he took in a terrifying experience. If the speaker of the poem considered the experience further, he could describe it rationally, but this he refused to do. For neither love nor money would he destroy his imagination by rationalizing it. Poe's careful revisions were lost on contemporary readers. He gave away some copies of the book but sold few.[28]

Poe reached West Point in the third week of June 1830 for the obligatory summer encampment, which even Ulysses S. Grant, who attended West Point the following decade, found 'very wearisome and uninteresting'.[29] When classes began in September, Poe took the same courses every first-year student took: French and Mathematics. Fellow cadet David Emerson Hale said Poe was 'too mad a poet to like Mathematics', but Poe himself would eventually recognize the importance of mathematics to poetry.[30]

Speaking with fellow cadets, Poe romanticized his past. He said he had been to South America and England and had graduated from an English college. Later, he romanticized his reason for leaving West Point. 'It was about this period that Poland made the desperate and unfortunate struggle for independence, against the combined powers of Russia, Austria and Prussia, which terminated in the capitulation of Warsaw, and the annihilation of the kingdom', Henry Hirst wrote. 'All our cadet's former chivalric ardor had now returned and with tenfold vigor. He burned to be a participant in the affray.' Poe's real reason for leaving West Point was less romantic. Frances Allan had passed away on 28 February 1829, and John Allan married Louisa Patterson on 5 October 1830. By the year's end the new Mrs Allan was pregnant. Realizing 'his heirship was at an end', Poe considered the army 'no place for a poor man'.[31] He quit attending classes, quit going to drill, quit doing pretty much everything the army ordered him to do. He was brought up on charges, courtmartialled and dismissed.

During his time at West Point, Poe endeared himself to his fellow cadets by writing satirical verse about their instructors. When he proposed a published collection of poems, the cadets readily subscribed.[32] Leaving West Point, he went to New York to oversee the volume's publication. By chance Peter Pease was there, too. Poe boisterously claimed he had made his fortune, acting the part of a prosperous gentleman and telling Pease he was living near Madison Square, where he 'loved to walk beneath the elm trees'.[33]

Poems (1831) begins with 'Letter to Mr —'. To make this collection less intimidating than his earlier ones, he moved 'Al Aaraaf' and 'Tamerlane' to the back. He added some fine new lyric poems, including 'To Helen', 'Irene', 'Israfel' and 'The City in the Sea'. *Poems* omits some minor works from the previous collections. In 'Letter to Mr —' Poe explains how he took some passages from the minor poems and integrated them with either 'Al Aaraaf' or 'Tamerlane', hoping to give them 'some chance of being seen by posterity'.[34] Preparing *Poems* for the publication, he saw his work as a matter of consolidation, taking the best lines from his minor poems and integrating them with his lengthier works.

'The Lake', for instance, disappears as a separate poem but reappears embedded within the text of 'Tamerlane'. After the revision, Tamerlane is the one remembering a lake he used to haunt in

Military Academy West Point.

his youth. A significant revision concerns the last four lines of the embedded poem. Whereas the speaker of 'The Lake' shifts to the third person to lament his lost youth, Tamerlane continues to speak in the first person, wondering:

> How could I from that water bring
> Solace to my imagining?
> My solitary soul – how make
> An Eden of that dim lake? (ll. 96–9)

The change removes much of the poem's complexity. Poe regretted it. He reverted to the 1829 version of 'Tamerlane' as the basis for later reprintings and made 'The Lake' a distinct work again.

The cadets did not like *Poems* at all. Assuming it would be filled with the satirical verse Poe had written at West Point, they were disappointed to find none of the poems they expected. Few copies reached the general public. A couple of mixed reviews appeared in the New York press, and Philadelphia editors reprinted selections. 'To Helen' appeared in *Atkinson's Saturday Evening Post*, and *Atkinson's Casket* reprinted 'To Helen', 'Irene' and 'Sonnet: To Science'.[35]

Edward J. Coale placed an advertisement for the book in the *Baltimore Gazette* the last week of April. That same week, the

Baltimore Patriot reviewed *Poems*. The reviewer took offence at Poe's position in 'Letter to Mr —', that 'none but poets are capable of forming a true estimate, or passing a correct judgment on poetry'. If that's the way Poe wanted it, so be it. The reviewer continued: 'Not, then, being poets, but belonging to the larger class thus challenged, we must profit by the monition, and carefully avoid expressing an opinion on the merits of the book.'[36] Presumably, Poe himself brought the extra copies of *Poems* with him from New York, so Coale's advertisement helps date his return to Baltimore.

Now living with Maria Clemm, Poe occasionally wrote to John Allan to beg for money. This summer Poe's future became even more tenuous. In Richmond on 23 August 1831, Louisa Allan gave her husband a legitimate heir, John Allan, Jr.

3

The Gothic Woman

'To dream has been the business of my life': so the nameless hero tells the narrator of 'The Visionary', the romantic tale Poe published in the January 1834 issue of *Godey's Lady's Book*. The hero is based on Lord Byron, but his statement reflects a personal ideal of the story's author. Poe very much wanted to make dreaming *his* lifelong pursuit, dreaming in the broadest sense of the term, a wide-awake dreaming that would fully utilize his mental powers. He wanted to explore the possibilities of his mind, testing the limits of his imagination to see how far he could take it.

John Allan's death in the last week of March 1834 changed Poe's dreams for good. Though Allan now had a legitimate heir, Poe still expected some kind of inheritance, one substantial enough to let him live comfortably and devote his life to literature. When Allan's will was probated the second week of May, Poe was stunned by his foster father's neglect. Allan had left him nothing. Poe suddenly faced a daunting future: he now had to rely on his pen for his livelihood. Besides Washington Irving and James Fenimore Cooper, no contemporary American author made a living solely as an author. For Poe, the situation was distasteful as well as intimidating. The world of the imagination, he naively believed, should be free from the crass and cut-throat world of business.

Poe's whereabouts for much of the year remains a mystery. Not until November did he inform John Pendleton Kennedy of his financial plight. He wrote to Kennedy because he was wondering if Henry

Carey might provide him an advance on *Tales of the Folio Club*. Since Kennedy had sent Poe's manuscript to him the previous November, Carey had held onto it without making a decision. Carey's behaviour seems unconscionable. If he did not want the book, he should have said so instead of stringing Poe along for a year.

Upon receiving Poe's letter, Kennedy again wrote Carey, who replied quickly this time. Though willing to publish *Tales of the Folio Club,* he did not expect to profit from it. Considering the book's unlikely prospects, he hesitated to pay its author an advance. Instead, Carey said Poe could turn a better profit by offering his tales to the annual gift books. A few years earlier Carey's quondam business partner Isaac Lea had suggested much the same to Poe, who had not taken advantage of the idea then due to his inexperience with the publishing world. This time Carey specifically recommended *The Gift*, the annual Eliza Leslie edited. Piecemeal publication of several stories in the annuals could generate more income than the publication of a single volume of tales.

Carey's hesitance to reject *Tales of the Folio Club* stemmed from his respect for Kennedy, not from indecisiveness. His comment about *The Gift* shows he was a shrewd businessman and a skilled publisher. He could look at a piece of writing, recognize where it belonged, and understand how to maximize income from it. Though disliking this dollars-and-cents approach to literature, Poe slowly realized he needed to become more business savvy if he ever hoped to profit from his writing. Disagreeable as it was, he needed to think about literature in terms of how much money he could make from it.

For one thing, he had to expand his audience. *Tales of the Folio Club*, after all, had been written for a very narrow readership: well-read individuals who could appreciate the subtlety of his satire. Poe had won the *Visiter* contest partly because he found in the committee – two lawyers and a physician – a group of intelligent, educated men well read in both ancient and modern literature, men who, like members of the fictional Folio Club, were wont to gather over good cigars and fine wine to discuss literature. There was a significant portion of the reading public Poe had yet to approach: women.

Publishing 'The Visionary' in *Godey's,* Poe took his first step toward exploiting this market. But he had not written 'The Visionary' specifically for women readers. Rather, he wrote it as part of *Tales of the Folio Club.* 'The Visionary' tells the story of a wealthy, handsome young romantic who loves the Marchesa Bianca, the beautiful wife of the old, cold-hearted Mentoni, but the story's sophistication stems from its narrative style. Despite their acquaintance, the narrator never fully understands the hero. He appreciates him as a dreamer and a poet without realising the depth of his love. The idea that a suicide pact would unite two lovers in a deeper, more spiritual love through the integration of their souls after death exceeds the narrator's comprehension.[1]

Poe hesitated to write specifically for *Godey's* or other women's magazines, an endeavour which, to his mind, would compromise his art. Moral tales and sentimental stories dominated the current market for women's fiction. Moral tales Poe refused to write: didactic fiction went against his most fundamental philosophy of art. He was ambivalent toward sentimentalism. He did not oppose it per se. Rather, he was against sentimentalism because its conventions had become clichés.

Poe's previously neglected copy of Susanna Rowson's *Charlotte Temple* – a classic example of literary sentimentalism – helps explain his ambivalence. The book's former owner, Elizabeth Poe, had inscribed the title page of the second volume when she obtained the book in 1807.[2] Her son inscribed his name directly beneath hers. The presence of his mother's signature softened Poe's attitude toward *Charlotte Temple* and the literature it represented. The book was a personal relic for Poe, a memento of the mother he had loved and lost at such a young age. Though she died before

Edgar's third birthday, his mother lived again whenever he opened *Charlotte Temple* and read her autograph.

The literary annuals provided another outlet for fiction and verse directed toward a predominantly female readership that Poe found more appealing than the women's magazines. On Kennedy's say-so, Carey sent the *Folio Club* manuscript to Eliza Leslie, who chose 'Manuscript Found in a Bottle' to include in *The Gift for 1836*. Happy with the dollar-per-page this fifteen-page story would bring, Poe did think republishing it in an annual was a mistake. Because the story had first appeared in 1833, it scarcely belonged in an annual for 1836. Instead, Poe thought, Leslie should have chosen one of his unpublished tales, say 'Epimanes' or 'Siope'.[3]

Though Poe's opinion of 'Epimanes' is overinflated, he correctly understood that 'Siope', a beautiful if cryptic prose poem, suited an annual gift book. A few years later he did publish it in an annual, *The Baltimore Book: A Christmas and New Year's Present*. Speaking of 'Siope', a reviewer of *The Baltimore Book* commented: 'This fable if we read it right, is intended to indicate the horror of silence – that man may not be entirely accursed while he can hear the sounds which hurtle in the bosom of nature; the curse of tumult is represented as happiness to the curse of silence. The strain is wild, the language beautiful and peculiar to Mr Poe.'[4]

The response to *The Gift for 1836* indicates Poe was right about republishing 'Manuscript Found in a Bottle' in an annual. The *Cincinnati Mirror*, which had reprinted the story from the Baltimore *Saturday Visiter* in 1833, reviewed *The Gift* two years later. The *Mirror* considered Poe 'a gentleman of very fine talents' and thought 'Manuscript Found in a Bottle' was 'wild and thrilling' but complained that an 1833 story did not belong in an annual for 1836.[5]

These remarks occur in a review of *Specimen of the Gift*, a sample copy of Leslie's annual issued in August and intended to give reviewers an indication of its contents. No copies of *Specimen of the Gift*

Mathew B. Brady,
Washington Irving,
1861.

survive, but this neglected review shows that Leslie recognized
Poe's literary talents and did what she could to further his career.
'Manuscript Found in a Bottle' was the only literary article *Specimen*
contained. In other words, Leslie used Poe's tale to demonstrate the
volume's overall quality. Her selection is especially notable since *The
Gift for 1836* would include contributions by several distinguished
authors: Washington Irving, James Kirke Paulding, Lydia Huntley
Sigourney and William Gilmore Simms.

The Washington Irving piece in *The Gift for 1836* was 'An
Unwritten Drama of Lord Byron', which relates the plot of a
tragedy Byron conceived but never wrote. A mysterious stranger
persistently follows a Spanish nobleman named Alfonso, who

becomes so perturbed that he fatally stabs the stranger – only to discover his own face on the victim. Irving suggested this plot provided 'a rich theme to a poet or dramatist of the Byron school'.[6]

Never one to back down from a challenge, Poe took Irving's suggestion to heart and used it as the basis for 'William Wilson'. This story had a long gestation period: Poe did not finish it until 1839, four years after reading Irving's sketch. Appropriately, he published 'William Wilson' in *The Gift for 1840*. Presenting a copy of his short story to Irving, Poe revealed another motive underlying its composition. He hoped Irving would 'find in it something to approve'.[7] The example of 'William Wilson' reflects a dual impulse that had been a part of Poe's make-up ever since John Allan took him in: he challenged the authority figures in his life while simultaneously seeking their approval.

Knowing he had to concentrate on writings that could make money, Poe still hesitated. As 1834 came to a close, he was working on *Politan*. The richly allusive quality of this closet tragedy has prompted one appreciative modern reader to call it 'an anthology of echoes', but *Politan* had little commercial appeal.[8] Kennedy discouraged Poe from it and got him 'drudging upon whatever may make money'.[9] He urged Poe to contribute to the *Southern Literary Messenger*, the monthly magazine Thomas W. White had started in Richmond that August. Poe soon completed 'Berenice' and sent it to White, who questioned its macabre conclusion but accepted the story nonetheless. 'Berenice' appeared in the March 1835 *Messenger*.

'Berenice' demonstrates what Poe had learned since publishing 'The Visionary'. Though a vivid example of Gothic literature, 'Berenice' has a basis in fact. It was inspired by a Baltimore scandal about grave-robbers digging up human remains to obtain teeth for dentists. Poe explained to White, 'The Tale originated in a bet that I could produce nothing effective on a subject so singular, provided I treated it seriously.'[10] Poe accepted the challenge and attempted a tale based on this gruesome subject.

Explaining his intentions, Poe told White, 'The history of all Magazines shows plainly that those which have attained celebrity were indebted for it to articles *similar in nature – to Berenice.*' Defining what he meant, he explained that the 'nature' of the story involved 'the ludicrous heightened into the grotesque: the fearful coloured into the horrible: the witty exaggerated into the burlesque: the singular wrought out into the strange and mystical'.[11] Poe's series of paired elements could be characterized by one more pair: the cliché rendered into the original. 'Berenice' shows he had found a way to alter the conventions of sentimental fiction to make them his own.

The story also marks a significant advance in Poe's narrative technique. More than that, 'Berenice' marks an advance in the general history of narrative. The narrator of 'The Visionary' is an aloof traveller, a person who observes what was happening, not the titular visionary who is the story's protagonist. Egaeus, the narrator of 'Berenice', tells his story from personal experience. Poe unites narrator and visionary in one individual. Suffering from monomania, Egaeus draws us into his world and lets us see things from his point of view. As the story of a diseased mind told from an inner perspective, 'Berenice' is Poe's first great psychological tale.

Though Egaeus and his cousin Berenice had grown up together, they seem like opposites. Whereas he is 'ill of health, and buried in gloom', she is 'agile, graceful, and overflowing with energy'.[12] Once illness overcomes her, she undergoes significant physical change, losing her athletic appearance. Her high forehead turns pale, and her temples become sunken. Her once golden hair turns raven black. (Poe would reverse the hair colour in a later revision.) Emaciated frame, high forehead, pale complexion, black hair: with the figure of Berenice, Poe created the Goth look.

Prior to her illness, Berenice's monomaniacal cousin had never fixated his attention on her, but when she smiles at him one day, he becomes obsessed with her teeth. Her sickness apparently leads to her death. The day she is interred, Egaeus blacks out for several hours, finding himself in his library late that evening. Unaware precisely what has transpired, he hears the echo of a piercing shriek and sees a mysterious box atop the nearby table. Egaeus slowly realizes he has disinterred Berenice and extracted her teeth. Such actions are frightful enough, but Poe is not finished. Berenice had been buried prematurely: she was still alive. The shriek echoes the sound she had made as he extracted her teeth.

White's misgivings about the denouement of 'Berenice' are understandable. Still, he recognized Poe's extraordinary talent and encouraged him to keep contributing. For the April 1835 issue White accepted 'Morella', the second story in what can be called Poe's Gothic woman trilogy. White also asked Poe to review several books for the April *Messenger*. The reviews display Poe's rapidly burgeoning critical skills; 'Morella' shows him developing his feminine ideal.

Morella shares Berenice's Gothic appearance. She has 'wan fingers', 'melancholy eyes' and a 'pale forehead'. She also suffers a life-threatening illness that accentuates her features: the sicker she gets, the more blue veins pop out on her forehead. Despite their physical similarities, Morella possesses two qualities Berenice lacks: a mind and a voice. Though the story's narrator does not love Morella, their intellectual life brings them together. They wed, and she becomes his mentor, sharing with him her passion for German mysticism. She has read deeply of John Locke and Johann Gottlieb Fichte, whose works concern the meaning of personal identity. Once sickness makes Morella hideous, the narrator reviles her.

With 'Morella', Poe breathed life into the biggest cliché of sentimental fiction: the tear-filled deathbed scene. Morella shows no emotion on her deathbed. Instead, she asserts her intellect, maintains her decorum and acknowledges her husband does not love her. As she dies, Morella gives birth to a daughter, who turns out to have her mother's mind, manner and look. Her father even names the girl after her.

American literature had never seen anything like 'Morella'. At a time when men occupied the public sphere and women were relegated to the private, domestic sphere, Poe brought husband and wife together in a shared intellectual world. He even made the wife intellectually superior to her husband. Because Morella dies the moment her daughter is born, Poe suggests that her soul has transmigrated, but this transfer of identity differs from the transmigration in 'Metzengerstein'. Morella's profound erudition, combined with her powerful will, assures her immortality. She is able to perpetuate her soul from one generation to the next because she has studied the meaning of identity and because her will is so strong it can transcend her physical existence.

Though 'Berenice' and 'Morella' incorporated elements of Gothic and sentimental fiction, both stories were too daring to achieve widespread contemporary acceptance. 'Lionizing', the next story Poe published in the *Southern Literary Messenger*, satirized, as Poe said later, 'the rage for Lions and facility of becoming one'.[13] Poe had written it as part of *Tales of the Folio Club*, but the spoof had a broad appeal. It tells the story of a young man with a large nose, which makes him the object of everyone's admiration. But when he shoots the nose off another in a duel, the newly noseless man assumes his place as the darling of society. Poe would carefully revise and republish this tale several times; he continually marvelled at how fickle the public could be. 'Hans Phaall', the pioneering work of science fiction Poe had drafted before 'Morella', appeared in the June *Messenger*.

On Tuesday, 7 July 1835, a real-life deathbed scene occurred in Maria Clemm's house as her seventy-nine-year-old mother breathed her last. The death evoked mixed emotions: sadness, relief, uncertainty. Caring for her paralytic mother had been a burden, but the old woman's government pension had allowed Maria to keep the household together. Without it, she could no longer afford to maintain the residence. Edgar would have to venture out on his own, and she and Virginia would have to move in with another relative, likely Edgar's second cousin Neilson Poe (pronounced Nelson). Edgar disliked this option, for he had fallen in love with his teenaged cousin. Frustrated with his inability to find a position in Baltimore, he relocated to Richmond.

A possible teaching job fell through, but White soon hired him to work at the *Messenger* full time. Though Poe considered himself the editor, White never assigned him that job title. Regardless, Poe performed an editor's work. He corresponded with contributors, prepared copy, proofread and wrote most of the reviews. Finally, he was on his way to being a journalist. The following month, however, he would almost destroy his budding career. Precisely what Poe said and did has escaped history, but the letters of White and Kennedy, combined with some general remarks by Lambert Wilmer, permit a conjectural account. Poe's alcoholism formed the

William James Bennet, *Richmond, from the Hill above the Waterworks*, 1834, engraved aquatint print based on a painting by George Cooke.

root of the problem. 'On some rare occasions', Wilmer observed, Poe 'was led astray by jovial companions and induced to join in their revels; and from the best information I can obtain, I judge that the use of intoxicating liquor had a maddening effect on him, inciting him to the most terrific acts of frenzy.'[14] One morning in mid-September 1835 proved to be such an occasion.

That morning Poe showed up at the *Messenger* office, scandalously drunk and ready to confront White. Precisely when Poe confronted his employer is uncertain, but morning makes a good conjecture. Afterwards, White admonished Poe: 'No man is safe who drinks before breakfast!'[15] Though Poe had only been with the *Messenger* for a few weeks, he had been reading it since White founded it the previous year. He had a good idea how to run the magazine, which was not how White was running it. In a drunken frenzy, Poe told White what he was doing wrong. Wilmer observed: 'It was one of his unfortunate tricks, when intoxicated, to insult his employer; or rather to make a statement of his grievances, which the employer was apt to think insulting.'[16] Shocked by this tirade, White dismissed him. Poe fled Richmond and returned to Baltimore.

Filled with remorse, he entered a state of profound melancholy. As White told a correspondent, 'I should not be at all astonished to hear that he has been guilty of suicide.'[17] According to Kennedy's correspondence, Poe did threaten to kill himself. After receiving a dark and despondent letter from Poe, Kennedy wrote back, urging him to put those 'villainous blue devils' behind him.[18]

Before the end of September, Poe wrote to White, pleading for another chance, insisting he had quit drinking for good. White was unconvinced. 'When you once again tread these streets', he responded, 'I have my fears that your resolves would fall through – and that you would again sip the juice, even till it stole away your senses.' Though hurt by Poe's angry remarks, White was generally fond of him and willing to help. He even offered Poe a room in his home: 'If you could make yourself contented to take up your quarters in my family, or in any other private family where liquor is not used, I should think there were hopes of you. – But, if you go to a tavern, or to any other place where it is used at table, you are not safe.'[19] White tentatively agreed to rehire Poe but promised to fire him if he ever got drunk again. Poe returned to Richmond ready to stay. Maria Clemm and her daughter Virginia joined him there. Initially, the three boarded with Mrs James Yarrington, but eventually Maria Clemm established a boarding-house of her own.

Poe's literary output for the next several months affirms his commitment to the *Messenger*. Time-consuming editorial duties prevented him from writing any new tales. All the short stories he published in the *Messenger* after 'Hans Phaall' were revised versions of ones he had written earlier as part of *Tales of the Folio Club*. His reviews show where most of his energy was going. White gave him considerable latitude when it came to reviewing books, and Poe took advantage of it. During his time with the *Messenger*, he started developing his unique critical voice. His uncompromising standards prompted the nickname 'Tomahawk Man', but he praised literature that deserved it. Augustus Baldwin Longstreet's anonymously published *Georgia Scenes*, for example, Poe welcomed with open arms: 'The author, whoever he is, is a clever fellow, imbued with a spirit of the truest humor, and endowed, moreover, with an exquisitely discriminative and penetrating understanding of *character* in general, and of Southern character in particular.'[20]

The most important review Poe published in the *Messenger* has become known as the 'Drake–Halleck Review', which appeared in the April 1836 issue. Examining the verse of two well-respected contemporary poets, Joseph Rodman Drake and Fitz Greene Halleck, Poe reversed popular opinion to put both men in their place. 'The Culprit Fay', Drake's most well-known poem, depicts a forest full of fairies wearing acorn helmets, carrying shields made from ladybird shells, using blades of grass for swords – the kind of fanciful forest creatures the Silly Symphonies cartoons revitalized in the twentieth century. Poe found much of Drake's description unintentionally humorous, especially the soldier crabs, the mailed shrimp and the spirits dressed in 'snail-plate armor'. Lifting Drake's description from its context, Poe lends it a surreal quality, a quality many of his short stories share. In fact, Salvador Dalí would call Poe 'the very frame of Surrealist reference'. Remembering a lively dinner conversation, Dalí said the subject of Edgar Allan Poe made 'a magnificent theme while savoring snails'.[21]

Drake had not meant 'The Culprit Fay' to be either humorous or surreal. As a serious work, however, it fell far short of fairy poems like Shelley's *Queen Mab*, as Poe recognized. Shelley enveloped his fairy in the 'moral sentiments of grace, of color, of motion – of the beautiful, of the mystical, of the august – in short of *the ideal*'. 'The Culprit Fay', alternatively, lacks an ideality of a high order. It is largely an incongruous assemblage of miscellaneous objects. Poe concluded: 'That we have among us poets of the loftiest order we believe – but we do not believe that these poets are Drake and Halleck.'[22]

Appearing in the same issue of the *Messenger* as the Drake–Halleck review, 'Maelzel's Chess-Player' shows another side of Poe's multifaceted talent. In this exposé, Poe revealed that Maelzel's renowned chess-playing automaton was an elaborate hoax. It was no machine but a carefully crafted cabinet that held a diminutive but highly skilled chess player inside. In an extraordinary assertion, Jean Cocteau named Poe the inventor of mass journalism, citing 'Maelzel's Chess-Player' as proof.[23] Cocteau essentially paralleled the workings of the Maelzel's pseudo-automaton with the mass media, hinting that what we read in our daily newspapers is controlled by invisible and unknown forces.

On Monday, 16 May 1836, Poe's life achieved a new-found level of stability when he and Virginia Clemm married. The ceremony, which took place at Mrs Yarrington's, was a quiet, understated affair. Besides the mother of the bride, only a few others attended.

Harper Brothers, *c.* 1860.

Thomas White and his daughter Eliza were there. So were Mr and
Mrs Thomas W. Cleland. Beforehand Mr Cleland testified that
Virginia was twenty-one years old. (Actually, she was not quite
fourteen.) The Reverend Amasa Converse officiated. A transplanted
Yankee who had studied at Dartmouth and Princeton before being
ordained a Presbyterian minister and coming south, Converse
found his true calling as a journalist. Poe knew him as the editor
of the Richmond *Southern Religious Telegraph.*

Despite their age difference (Poe was now twenty-seven), he and
Virginia made a handsome couple. Out walking around Richmond
soon after their marriage, they happened to meet Elmira Royster

Shelton. Now married with children, Elmira retained feelings for Edgar. It was hard for her to encounter the newlyweds. She recalled, 'I remember seeing Edgar, and his lovely wife, very soon after they were married – I met them – I never shall forget my feelings at the time – They were indescribable, almost agonizing.'[24]

Still hoping to publish *Tales of the Folio Club*, Poe sought Paulding's help to place the book with Harpers. Paulding had less influence than Poe assumed. He could not convince Harpers to publish the *Tales of the Folio Club*. Since the tales had already appeared in the magazines, they lacked novelty. A longer, book-length narrative was more marketable than a collection of short stories. Though Poe gave *Tales of the Folio Club* unity by creating a narrative framework and bridging the stories with burlesque criticism, the work could not pass muster as a single narrative. Republished magazine articles, Harpers told Poe, 'are the most unsaleable of all literary performances'.[25]

Though he had no particular desire to write a book-length work of fiction, Poe took Harpers' suggestion as a challenge and began drafting *The Narrative of Arthur Gordon Pym*. Before releasing Pym separately, he decided to publish it serially. One instalment appeared in the January 1837 *Messenger*, another the following month. Poe had done what the publishers told him to do: he had written a sustained narrative long enough to fill an entire volume. Harpers accepted the work in 1837, copyrighted it, and advertised its forthcoming publication.

Poe quit the *Messenger* before the second instalment of *Pym* appeared. Frustrated with the paltry wages he received – ten dollars a week – he could not convince his employer to give him a raise. His growing national reputation let him think he could obtain a better editorial position elsewhere. Francis L. Hawks, a contributor to the *New York Review*, wrote, 'I wish you to fall in with your *broad-axe* amidst this miserable literary trash which surrounds us.'[26] Poe misinterpreted Hawks's wishful thinking as an actual job offer. In January 1837 he left Richmond for New York in January 1837 with his wife and mother-in-law.

They found an apartment at Sixth Avenue and Waverley Place, where they shared a floor with William Gowans, a rare book dealer who became friends with the family and fueled Poe's interest in 'quaint and curious volumes of forgotten lore'. Poe also befriended the eminent classical scholar Charles Anthon. Asked to review John Stephens's *Incidents of Travel in Egypt, Arabia Petraea, and the Holy Land*, Poe approached Anthon for help with some of the book's Hebrew phrases. Thomas Jefferson was right: University of Virginia students did need to know Hebrew. Poe even had the opportunity to visit Anthon's home. Impressed with his personal library, Poe noted that Anthon's 'love of elegance' prompted him 'to surround himself, in his private study, with gems of sculptural art and beautifully bound volumes, all arranged with elaborate attention to form, and in the very pedantry of neatness'.[27] Professor Anthon's luxurious lifestyle was one Poe could only dream of living.

In the last week of March Poe, Gowans, Anthon and many other important litterateurs attended the booksellers' banquet at the City

Broadway, New York, 1836.

Dr Charles Anthon, *c.* 1860.

Hotel. The attendees devoted hours to formal and informal toasts. Toward the evening's end, Poe stood up, offering a somewhat self-serving toast to the '*Monthlies* of Gotham – Their distinguished Editors, and their vigorous Collaborateurs'. Poe came away from the event with great hope for his career. His plans seemed to be falling into place. With such enthusiastic support, the world of literature seemed destined to flourish. All that would soon change.[28]

Though Harpers planned to publish *Pym* in 1837, an economic event of nationwide significance intervened. In April businesses failed almost daily. Adverse economic conditions precipitated the 'Panic of 1837', which marked one of the worst depressions in American history. The land boom, which had lasted a dozen years, collapsed. Across the nation, banks failed and factories closed. Every industry was affected – including the publishing industry.

Harpers curtailed their new publications, withdrawing works that were not surefire hits. *Pym* was withheld from publication.

Other authors were affected by the depression. Harpers discontinued its multi-volume edition of Paulding's collected works. Poe could take heart knowing he was in good company, but Harpers' decision to stop publication of Paulding's works sent the message that a well-established name was no guarantee of continued success. Though disappointed with the decision, Paulding did not rely on his pen for survival. The setback had no effect on his career. He reached the pinnacle of his profession the next year when President Martin Van Buren appointed him Secretary of the Navy.[29]

From the time Poe's review of Stephens's *Incidents of Travel* appeared in October 1837 until the middle of the following year, little evidence survives to document his whereabouts. By the third week of July 1838, Harpers had yet to release *Pym*, and Poe had exhausted the possibilities for employment in New York. He and his family left for Philadelphia. Poe wrote Paulding, asking him for a clerical position with the US Navy: 'Could I obtain the most unimportant Clerkship in your gift – *any thing, by sea or land* – to relieve me from the miserable life of literary drudgery to which I, now, with a breaking heart, submit, and for which neither my temper nor my abilities have fitted me?'[30] By the summer of 1838 Poe was at his nadir and ready to abandon the literary life. Before the end of July Harpers finally released *The Narrative of Arthur Gordon Pym*.

Philadelphia did not have much to offer in terms of literary employment. James Pedder, a popular children's author, found Poe and his family living 'on bread and molasses for weeks together' and 'literally suffering for want of food'.[31] *Pym*, which met with mixed reviews, provided little income. In hard times, magazines hesitated to pay contributors. With few opportunities to publish tales in the periodicals, Poe's development as an author of short fiction had been on hold for three years. 'Hans Phaall' was the last original story he had published. Though he had published it in

1835, its composition dates back to the previous year. 'Morella' had been the last story Poe had written. Asked to contribute to a new magazine in 1838, Poe picked up where he had left off. 'Ligeia', as he titled this story, revisits a theme he had introduced in 'Berenice' and developed in 'Morella'.

In some ways 'Ligeia' is a redaction of 'Morella'. Both tales are narrated by husbands whose wives look alike and think alike. Furthermore, each contracts a fatal illness and seemingly returns from death in different form, largely through the dual power of intellect and will. But key differences separate the two stories. The description in 'Ligeia', simultaneously vague yet ornate, surpasses that of 'Morella'. Poe took great pleasure in the newer story's complexity. Eight years later he still considered 'Ligeia' his best story.[32]

Poe's use of ambiguity in 'Ligeia' contributes to its richness. Morella's supernatural return in the figure of her daughter must be taken at face value. The return of Ligeia in the body of the Lady Rowena is more ambiguous. It may be supernatural, but there are alternate ways to explain the transformation. Perhaps the narrator, his mind addled by opium, is hallucinating. The resemblance between Rowena's bridal chamber and a phantasmagoria show – a form of popular entertainment in Poe's day – presents another way to explain what happens in 'Ligeia'. Phantasmagoria shows often featured at least one transformation, during which a projected image of one person would be transformed into another. Rowena's final resemblance to Ligeia could be the result of a similar optical illusion. Black magic may also play a part. Rowena's bridal chamber is shaped like a pentagram, the traditional five-sided figure used to cast spells and make curses. Suggesting all these possibilities, and more, to explain Ligeia's return in the form of Rowena, Poe let his readers decide, creating a tale that would continue to captivate and beguile. With 'Ligeia', Poe made the Gothic woman timeless.

4

Making a Name

'Ligeia' appeared in the first issue of the *American Museum of Science, Literature, and the Arts*, a monthly edited by two of Poe's Baltimore friends, Nathan C. Brooks and Dr Joseph E. Snodgrass, which premiered in September 1838. Poe had several reasons for publishing his story here. Unable to find a new editorial position himself, he needed other outlets for his work, and, as always, he desperately needed money. But he had reasons beyond self-interest for placing 'Ligeia' with the *American Museum*. He wanted to help his friends launch the magazine with style and hoped to encourage the development of American periodical literature by example. Brooks and Snodgrass, in turn, had similar reasons for asking Poe to contribute. Knowing he was in dire straits, they hoped to help him. The ten dollars they paid for 'Ligeia' temporarily relieved Poe from destitution.[1] But they wanted to establish a successful, high-quality magazine, too. They recognized Poe as one of the nation's finest authors *and* one of its most controversial literary figures. The reputation Poe had developed at the *Southern Literary Messenger* remained fresh in the minds of American readers. Brooks and Snodgrass knew Poe's name would help sell magazines.

They rightly foresaw its market value. Nathaniel Parker Willis applauded the first issue of the *American Museum* in his column in George P. Morris's *New-York Mirror*, but Poe was the only contributor he mentioned specifically.[2] Poe himself had long been aware of the importance of establishing a name for himself. When Henry

Carey told him in the mid-1830s that if he could 'obtain anything like a name' he would find it easier to get a book published, he was not telling him anything new. Trying to convince John Allan to subvent the publication of *Al Aaraaf, Tamerlane, and Minor Poems* in 1829, Poe explained, 'At my time of life there is much in being *before the eye of the world* – if once noticed I can easily cut out a path to reputation.'[3] In 'Letter to Mr —', Poe observed, 'It is with literature as with law or empire – an established name is an estate in tenure, or a throne in possession.'[4] While at the *Messenger*, he solicited contributions from James Fenimore Cooper and other prominent authors for a special issue 'consisting altogether of articles from distinguished Americans, whose *names* may give weight and character to this work'.[5]

Brooks solicited additional contributions from Poe for the *American Museum*. He especially wanted a review of Washington Irving's works. It is a testament to Poe's literary integrity that he declined. Feeling he could not write the review in the time frame Brooks gave him, he turned the offer down, turning down, too, the remuneration he would have received for it. He did suggest a possible approach: 'Irving is much overrated, and a nice distinction might be drawn between his just and his surreptitious and adventitious reputation – between what is due to the pioneer solely, and what to the writer.'[6]

Poe's refusal to write quickly for the sake of a few more dollars indicates the care he took in shaping his literary reputation. Despite the nagging poverty, he hesitated to risk his name with anything less than his best. Having started to make his name at the *Messenger*, he wanted to sustain and expand it. But what did establishing a name really mean? Poe pondered the question himself in a story he published in the November issue of the *American Museum*: 'The Psyche Zenobia'.

'Keenly sarcastic and exquisitely humorous', according to one contemporary reviewer, 'The Psyche Zenobia' is better known in revised form as 'How to Write a Blackwood Article'.[7] Both versions parody the characteristic style of articles from *Blackwood's Edinburgh Magazine*. As a parody, 'The Psyche Zenobia' marks a vast improvement over Poe's earlier *Blackwood's* spoof, 'A Decided Loss', which is better known in revised form as 'Loss of Breath'. Whereas 'A Decided Loss' had taken for granted the reader's familiarity with *Blackwood's*, 'The Psyche Zenobia' makes no such assumptions. Instead, it satirically defines the Blackwood style before spoofing it. Ultimately, the story scrutinizes what it means to have a personal name so closely associated with a particular literary style.

Poe split 'The Psyche Zenobia' into two parts. In the first, the title character, who is also the narrator, leaves her native Philadelphia for a trip to Edinburgh to meet the famous Mr Blackwood and learn how to write in the Blackwood style. The second part, titled 'The Scythe of Time' (better known in revised form as 'A Predicament'), presents a story she has written based on his principles.

'The Psyche Zenobia' starts with the narrator identifying herself: 'I presume everybody has heard of me. My name is the Signora Psyche Zenobia. This I know to be a fact. Nobody but my enemies ever call me Suky Snobbs.'[8] She then begins a long-winded explanation of the meaning of the name 'Psyche' but interrupts herself to blame Tabitha Turnip for spreading a rumour that her real name is Suky. Her defensive attitude suggests that her name really is Suky and that Psyche Zenobia is an invention. Having carefully constructed this public identity, she now wants to sustain it, even within her private circle of acquaintances.

Though Psyche guards her personal identity at first, she soon seems willing to sacrifice it for the sake of her literary style. Having been assured that the finest writing appears in *Blackwood's*, she now wants to write 'an article of the genuine Blackwood stamp'. When she meets Mr Blackwood, he uses similar language to characterize the style of his magazine's articles. He tells her to 'pay minute attention to the sensations'. Only then can she compose 'what may be denominated a genuine Blackwood article of the sensation stamp'.[9] Satirizing the literary style associated with *Blackwood's*, Poe questions whether a magazine's publisher should determine a contributor's style. Must authors sacrifice their individuality for the sake of getting published?

Taking Mr Blackwood's advice, Psyche considers different sensations she might describe. When she suggests hanging herself with a pair of garters and then describing how it felt, he tells her that hanging has become clichéd. His comment forms an example of self-parody on Poe's part. Revising 'A Decided Loss' into 'Loss of Breath', he had added a lengthy passage describing the sensations of a man being hanged. Instead of hanging herself, he suggests she take a dose of Morrison's pills and then describe her sensations. Morrison's pills were a popular cure-all in the 1830s, but some people self-medicated so thoroughly they poisoned themselves. Poe's nurse friend Mary Louise Shew knew a man with a pill mania who took Morrison's pills for every little ailment and accidentally killed himself.[10] To keep the story current, Poe changed his reference to Brandeth's pills in its revised version. The revision shows how quickly brand names could date.

At first glance, Poe's reference to Morrison's pills seems nothing more than a satirical jab at a popular fad, but the phrase – a possessive form of a proper name linked to a commercial product – sounds strangely familiar. Structurally the phrase 'Morrison's pills' is identical to 'Blackwood's magazine'. Both the pills and the magazine are products endorsed and sanctioned by their originator and proprietor. When magazine contributors write according to identical principles, then their articles become, so to speak, nothing more than drugs on the market.

In 'The Scythe of Time', Psyche Zenobia relates how she leaves Mr Blackwood's Edinburgh office in search of sensations, climbs a clock steeple and pokes her head from a hole in the clockface. The minute hand soon presses upon Psyche's neck, first popping out her eyeballs and then severing her head but never preventing her from seeing or thinking. (At times, Poe's clocks could be more surreal than Dalí's.) The experience gives her many sensations to describe and much to ponder: 'With my head I imagined, at one time, that I the head, was the real Signora Psyche Zenobia – at another I felt convinced that myself, the body, was the proper identity.'[11] Despite the outrageous humour, Zenobia's words reflect a serious purpose, one that runs through much of Poe's *oeuvre*: the meaning of identity. Can the body retain its identity even after a part has been severed from it? Perhaps Psyche's decapitation literalizes what she has already done figuratively. By choosing to write in the Blackwood manner, she has already sacrificed her personal identity.

Around the time 'The Psyche Zenobia' appeared, Poe offered his name to Thomas Wyatt, who used it for *The Conchologist's First Book*. Poe's textual contributions to Wyatt's book display none of his characteristic literary style. He contributed to the book solely for the fifty dollars Wyatt offered him. This sum provided welcome relief, but Poe could not continue relying on piecework to survive. He needed steady employment. In May 1839, the month *The Conchologist's First Book* appeared, he approached William E. Burton for a job.

Born and raised in England, Burton had developed a fine reputation as a comedian on the London stage. In 1834 he settled in the us and became 'the reigning king of comedy in America'.[12] With a lifelong ambition to edit a magazine, he took advantage of his celebrity status to gather magazine subscriptions. He also interested Charles Alexander, the publisher of *Alexander's Weekly Messenger*, in the venture. With Alexander as publisher and Burton as editor, the *Gentleman's Magazine* was launched in 1837. Two years later Burton bought out Alexander and changed the title to *Burton's Gentleman's Magazine*. The new title reinforced Burton's association with the periodical, further helped him capitalize on his fame, and let him brand the magazine as his own.

William E. Burton, *c.* 1855.

Burton recognized Poe's talents and agreed to take him on as assistant editor, a magnanimous gesture in light of his severe critique of *The Narrative of Arthur Gordon Pym* the previous year. In his review, Burton had observed, 'We regret to find Mr Poe's name in connexion with such a mass of ignorance and effrontery.'[13] Since Burton greatly appreciated the critical work Poe had done for the *Southern Literary Messenger*, he regretted Poe's role in a fictional narrative purporting truth. From Burton's perspective, *The Narrative of Arthur Gordon Pym* damaged the name Poe had made for himself at the *Messenger*.

Their working relationship got off to a rocky start. The first item Poe wrote for Burton was a scathing retrospective of contemporary poet Rufus Dawes. Burton refused to publish it, encouraging Poe to treat fellow authors with camaraderie: 'We shall agree very well, but you must get rid of your avowed ill-feelings towards your brother-authors.' Since, in Burton's opinion, the magazine had already established a reputation for its independent book reviews, there was no need for undue criticism.[14] I welcome your help, Burton essentially said, but do not forget whose name is in the magazine's title. Burton set a convivial tone for its reviews, an approach that prevented Poe from cultivating his unique critical voice.

A frequent contributor to *Burton's*, Thomas Dunn English met Poe for the first time at the magazine's office. The two would later quarrel viciously, but Poe made a good initial impression on English, whose recollection provides a good picture of Poe at this time in his life:

I was impressed favorably with the appearance and manner of the author. He was clad in a plain and rather worn suit of black which was carefully brushed, and his linen was especially notable for its cleanliness. His eyes at that time were large, bright and piercing, his manner easy and refined, and his tone and conversation winning. In a short while we went out of the office together and remained in conversation as we walked along the street. We parted in Chestnut Street some few blocks above Third, apparently well pleased with each other.[15]

When the June 1839 issue of *Burton's* announced Poe's association with the magazine, his name caught the attention of other magazinists. The editor of the Philadelphia *Saturday Courier*, for one, commented: 'Mr. Poe was very favourably known as editor of the *Southern Literary Messenger* in its early days; and he has produced several works, which prove him a man of letters and industry. His accession is very valuable.'[16] Speaking of Poe, Charles Alexander said, 'He is a gentleman of superior ability and character, and we are glad to see that his name is associated with Mr Burton in the future direction of the *Gentleman's Magazine*.'[17]

Working for *Burton's*, Poe chose submissions, contributed verse, prepared manuscripts, proofread copy, supervised production at the printers and, in short, did everything involved with editing the magazine. Though the tight control Burton exercised over the review section frustrated Poe, Burton was doing him a favour. By preventing Poe from committing too much thought to criticism, Burton gave him the opportunity to channel his energy into his fiction. While working for Burton, Poe wrote some of the best tales of his career. The August issue of *Burton's* includes 'The Man that was Used Up: A Tale of the Late Bugaboo and Kickapoo Campaign'. This story continues to work the humourous vein Poe had mined with 'The Psyche Zenobia'. He even included a recurring character to link the two tales. Tabitha T of 'The Man that was Used Up' bears a striking resemblance to Tabitha Turnip. In addition to its use of humour, this new tale also resembles 'The Psyche Zenobia' as it explores the relationship between name and identity.

'The Man that was Used Up' tells the story of Brevet Brigadier General John A.B.C. Smith. Despite his common name, General Smith is a fine figure of a man with a distinguished air about him and a distinguished career behind him. Curious about the general, the story's narrator approaches different people on different occasions to learn more. He anticipates the reporter in *Citizen Kane*, who approaches Charlie Kane's friends to understand him, only to be frustrated in his quest. When people try to tell the narrator something about General Smith in 'The Man that was Used Up', their conversations get interrupted, and he walks away dissatisfied.

He gradually recognizes the impossibility of knowing someone solely by reputation and decides to see General Smith in person. Shown into the general's chamber while he is dressing, the narrator notices on the floor 'a large and exceedingly odd-looking bundle'. As he kicks it aside, the strange bundle addresses him in a funny little voice. Soon, Pompey, General Smith's servant, hands the bundle a prosthetic leg, which it screws on, thus enabling it to stand. The bundle *is* the general. Next Pompey screws on General Smith's prosthetic arm. The general speaks to the narrator as he gets himself together. 'Thomas', he recommends, 'is decidedly the best hand at a cork leg; but if you should ever want an arm, my dear fellow, you must let me recommend you to Bishop.'[18] As Pompey supplies the manufactured body parts, the general mentions the brand names of each: Pettit for shoulders, Ducrow for bosoms, De L'Orme for wigs, Parmly's for teeth, Dr Williams for eyes, Bonfanti's for the palate.

In 'The Man that was Used Up', General Smith provides a counterpoint for the emerging concept of the self-made man in American culture. Smith is a product of the age of invention, which he personally praises. As Psyche Zenobia had questioned her own identity upon being decapitated, 'The Man that was Used Up' questions the very meaning of identity. How much of ourselves can we lose and still retain our personal identity? General Smith has lost so much of himself that the fact of his loss now defines him.

The general's emphasis on the brand names of his various prosthetics makes a comment on modern consumer culture. Much as people nowadays buy name-brand clothing, timepieces and other personal accessories as status symbols, General Smith drops the names of his body parts to emphasize their quality. He relies on these name-brand products to construct his personal identity.

Another film analogy: when Mireille Darc loses her Hermès handbag in an auto accident in Jean-Luc Godard's *Week End,* she feels such a sense of loss that she is willing to risk her life in a burning auto to retrieve it. Those who use brand names to construct their personal identity must guard their possessions for fear of losing themselves. General Smith, too, has constructed his identity from name-brand products. Without them, he is a man who has been used up, nothing more than a nondescript bundle others can easily kick around.

Poe's contributions to *Burton's* greatly enhanced the magazine's quality. 'The Fall of the House of Usher', which many consider his finest tale, appeared in September 1839 to widespread acclaim. John Frost, editor of *Alexander's,* praised the story, calling it 'a noble and imposing picture, such as can be drawn only by a master hand. Such things are not produced by your slip-shod amateurs in composition.'[19] Poe, who worked hard throughout his career to emphasize literature as a professional pursuit, found such words especially gratifying. Frost also appreciated 'William Wilson', which appeared in *Burton's* the following month. He recognized the tale's pictorial quality, too, suggesting that Poe 'paints with sombre Rembrandt-like tints'.[20]

Both 'The Fall of the House of Usher' and 'William Wilson' are highly complex works, neither of which can be reduced to a single interpretation. Like Poe's other tales of the late 1830s, both play upon the theme of personal identity. Instead of using the idea of dismemberment as he does elsewhere, Poe splits an individual identity between two characters in both of these stories. 'William Wilson', the greatest doppelgänger tale in American literature, gives one man an evil nature and the other a moral sense and explores their interrelationship. Similarly, Roderick Usher and his twin sister Madeline represent two halves of a single identity, which only achieves unity in death. These two thought-provoking and carefully crafted tales question to what an extent any individual can integrate the opposing parts of the self.

A frame enlargement of James Sibley Watson and Melville Webber's *The Fall of the House of Usher*.

To enhance the prestige of *Burton's Gentleman's Magazine* further, Poe and Burton devised a contest like no previous one in the history of American journalism. According to their announcement, which appeared in November 1839, the contest would award premiums totalling a thousand dollars. There would be eight separate awards ranging from fifty dollars for a sketch of foreign travel to two hundred and fifty for a series of five tales. The contest attracted submissions from Boston to Baltimore. James Russell Lowell, then a law student at Harvard, entered the contest. So did Joseph Snodgrass.

Poe later wrote to Snodgrass, telling him the contest was all Burton's idea.[21] But Poe's letters do not always make the best biographical evidence. As Geoffrey Rans observes, 'In his letters he dramatizes himself to such an extent that the truth is hard to come by.'[22] The details of the contest suggest that Burton welcomed

Poe's input. The reward for the set of tales indicates the importance Poe placed on story cycles. And the explanation of the judging process reflects Poe's attitude toward literary professionalism:

> The Editors do not intend to insult the competitors by referring their productions to the scrutiny of 'a committee of literary gentlemen', who generally select, unread, the effusion of the most popular candidate as the easiest method of discharging their onerous duties. Every article sent in will be carefully perused by the Editors alone – and as they have hitherto catered successfully for the taste of their readers, and daily sit in judgment upon literary matters connected with the Review department, it is supposed that they possess sufficient capability to select the worthiest production offered to their notice.[23]

Poe was greatly disappointed when Burton cancelled the contest the following year. In retrospect, Burton seemed disingenuous. He just advertised it as a publicity stunt while never intending to fulfil his promise, Poe concluded. The matter of the contest caused a chasm to open in the professional relationship between Burton and Poe.

Though increasingly dissatisfied with different aspects of the magazine, Poe could not deny that his continued association with *Burton's* was helping him build his name. His ongoing notoriety finally led to the publication of a collected edition of his short stories, *Tales of the Grotesque and Arabesque*. The edition is dated 1840, but publisher Lea and Blanchard issued the book in December 1839. A landmark in American literary history, *Tales of the Grotesque and Arabesque* was less a triumph for Poe than it seems now. Beforehand, his publisher told him it did not expect to profit from the book and would issue it solely as a personal favour. After originally agreeing to publish 1750 copies, the firm scaled back the edition, publishing only 750 copies.[24]

Poe's dealings with Lea and Blanchard embittered him toward the literary marketplace. The world of business, which was coming to define American society, upset and dismayed Poe. In early 1840 he launched a satirical attack on a new type of person who was emerging as a major force in American culture, the businessman. The term 'businessman' had only recently entered the English language, but Poe's short story, 'Peter Pendulum, The Business Man', codified, albeit satirically, the defining characteristics of the type. Poe first published the story in the February 1840 issue of *Burton's*. He later revised and greatly expanded it, changing the title to 'The Business Man' and changing the name of his narrator-protagonist to Peter Proffit.

Whether named Peter Pendulum or Peter Proffit, Poe's character exemplifies the traits of the American businessman, who shifts from one frivolous endeavour to another to make a buck. The story applies as much today as it did in the 1840s. The stereotypical businessman switches careers frequently, always looking for a better opportunity. Devoid of aesthetic sensibilities, he thinks nothing of uglying up the town for the sake of profit. He also seems willing to sacrifice his personal identity for money. In Peter Proffit's case, making a buck becomes more important than making a name. Wearing the clothing of the tailors who employ him, he sacrifices his personal identity and transforms himself into a mannequin. Like General Smith, he becomes a walking advertisement for the products he wears.

While working for Burton, Poe also contributed to *Alexander's Weekly Messenger*. His anonymous contributions treat a variety of subjects from beetroot to bloodhounds, revivals to railroads. 'Enigmatical and Conundrum-ical', his earliest known contribution to *Alexander's*, challenges readers to submit cryptograms for him to solve, the harder the better. Submissions were soon forthcoming. Poe rose to the challenge and solved several puzzles. He ultimately quit solving puzzles for *Alexander's*, not because they got too difficult but because they grew too numerous. He would later demonstrate his cryptographic skills in *Graham's Magazine* and make a cryptographic puzzle an essential part of 'The Gold-Bug'.

Poe's interest in cryptography reflects a broader issue that forms a prominent motif in his fiction: how can the apparent hold hidden messages? He was inspired by another neglected work that formed a part of his modest personal library, *Select Pieces on Commerce, Natural Philosophy, Morality, Antiquities, History, &c.* (1754).[25] This anthology of mid-eighteenth-century magazine articles contains an essay by Willem Jacob 's Gravesande about coded messages, presenting different forms of secret writing and showing how to decipher them. 'The Gold Bug', in turn, inspired another prominent cryptographer, Leo Marks, head of agents' codes and ciphers at Special Operations Executive (SOE) during World War II. Marks decided to become a cryptographer after he encountered 'The Gold Bug' as a boy at his father's antiquarian bookshop at 84 Charing Cross Road. He was also indebted to Poe's psychological tales of terror: Marks would later write the screenplay for Michael Powell's *Peeping Tom*.

'The Daguerreotype', perhaps the most important article Poe contributed to *Alexander's*, presents an appreciation of the newly invented process of photography. Years would pass before the photogravure process emerged, but the invention of the daguerreotype contributed to the proliferation of engraved portraiture. Formerly, engravings had been based on paintings, but now they could be patterned on photographs. Editors encouraged authors to have daguerreotypes taken so that their portraits could be published with their writings. Suddenly, establishing a literary reputation not only involved making a name, it also involved cultivating a personal image.

As a weekly magazine, *Alexander's* was not in direct competition with the monthlies, so Burton did not mind Poe's contributions to it. Actually, Poe used the pages of *Alexander's* to promote *Burton's*. In one contribution, Poe called the issue of *Burton's* containing 'Peter Pendulum' 'one of the best specimens, if not the very best specimen, of a monthly Magazine, which has yet been issued in this country'.[26] Poe also contributed to the *Daily Chronicle*, the newspaper Alexander published. In May 1840 he published brief appreciations of two fellow authors, F. W. Thomas and Jesse Erskine Dow, in the *Chronicle*. These articles provide a clue to what was happening in Poe's personal life this month.

Before meeting Dow personally, Poe knew him as the author of 'Sketches from the Log of Old Ironsides', a series of articles that had appeared in *Burton's* over the previous nine months. Dow's sketches were based on his personal experience as private secretary to Commodore Jesse Duncan Elliot aboard the *US Constitution*. Now working as a clerk in the Post Office Department in Washington, Dow came to Philadelphia in May 1840 as a witness in Elliot's court martial. While in town, he naturally sought out the man who had supervised the publication of his sketches.

This same month Poe also met Cincinnati novelist F. W. Thomas. Poe had reviewed *Clinton Bradshaw*, Thomas's first novel, for the *Southern Literary Messenger*. Thomas came to Philadelphia this May seeking a publisher for his new novel, *Howard Pinckney.* He greatly respected Poe's opinion and sought him out in Philadelphia. Poe apparently met Thomas soon after meeting Dow and introduced the two men. All three became fast friends, often gathering to discuss literature at the hotel kept by John Sturdivant at the corner of Chestnut and Third Streets next door to Congress Hall.

It is impossible to know exactly what the three said to each other at Sturdivant's hotel, but a letter from Poe to Thomas fondly recalls 'those literary and other disquisitions about which we quarrelld at Studevant's'.[27] Thomas's memory of their conversations reflects similar sentiments, though he often listened while Poe and Dow spoke: 'It was delightful to hear the two talk together and to see how Poe would start at some of Dow's "strange notions" as he called them.'[28]

Poe candidly expressed his opinion about *Howard Pinckney*, evaluating it in terms of Thomas's reputation:

> You give yourself up to your own nature (which is a noble one, upon my soul) in Clinton Bradshaw; but in Howard Pinckney you abandon the broad rough road for the dainty by-paths of authorism. In the former you are interested in what you write and write to please, pleasantly; in the latter, having gained a name, you write to maintain it, and the effort becomes apparent ... If you would send the public opinion to the devil, forgetting that a public existed, and writing from the natural promptings of your own spirit you would do wonders.[29]

Poe's advice reveals the danger involved after an author establishes a name: stagnation. Once an author gets known for a certain style, the reading public expects him or her to continue writing in that same style. By doing so, authors can sustain their initial reputation. To progress as an artist, however, an author must experiment with different approaches, different styles. Making a name is not enough: an author must be willing to put that name on the line with each new work.

While serving as assistant editor at *Burton's*, Poe began planning his own monthly magazine. He was not trying to compete with Burton directly. Poe did not circulate a prospectus announcing his own journal until after Burton announced the sale of his magazine. Assuming that Poe's venture would diminish the market value of *Burton's Gentleman's Magazine* and adversely affect the profit that could be realized on its sale, Burton angrily dismissed Poe in the last week of May 1840.

The dismissal meant the end of 'The Journal of Julius Rodman', a fictional narrative relating the story of a journey across North

America that supposedly antedated the Lewis and Clark expedition. Poe had been serializing the narrative in *Burton's*, but he now abandoned it. He did not mind the loss of 'Julius Rodman' much. His heart had never been in the project. He had begun it mainly as a way to fill up space in *Burton's*; he had borrowed big chunks of text from previous works of Western travel without acknowledgement. The problems with the lengthy 'Journal of Julius Rodman' reinforced the aesthetic of short fiction Poe was evolving.[30]

The dismissal put Poe in desperate financial straits, but it gave him time to pursue his own magazine more aggressively. He planned to call it the *Penn Magazine*. In the prospectus, he reminded readers of his critical notices in the *Southern Literary Messenger*. He emphasized the importance of a rigorous review department. For those readers who formerly found Poe's critical voice too harsh, he explained: 'One or two years, since elapsed, may have mellowed down the petulance, without interfering with the rigor of the critic.' The creative department in the magazine would exemplify Poe's aesthetic. Imaginative literature would delight, not instruct: 'It will leave the task of instruction in better hands. Its aim, chiefly, shall be *to please*; and this through means of versatility, originality and pungency.' Poe emphasized the importance of a strong magazine editor. Unlike Blackwood, however, he would not determine the style of the tales and verse he published. Poe's critical terms – 'versatility', 'originality' – emphasize that contributors would be free to develop their own unique voices.

Poe told a correspondent he hoped his new magazine would 'produce some lasting effect upon the growing literature of the country', but also that it would establish a name for himself that the nation 'will not willingly let die'.[31] Though hoping the magazine would make his name, the title Poe chose for it reinforces his decision to let his contributors cultivate their individual abilities. Unlike *Alexander's* or *Blackwood's* or *Burton's*, Poe would not name his magazine after himself. In other words, he would not use his own name to brand the literature that appeared in his magazine. Calling his planned magazine after the state where he lived (and punning on the word 'pen'), Poe would let the writers who contributed to it make names for themselves.

5

From Peeping Tom to Detective

Tales of the Grotesque and Arabesque was not published outside the
USA, but a few copies circulated in other English-speaking parts of
the world soon after its publication. Poe presented one to Charles
Dickens. Australian bookman Nicol D. Stenhouse somehow managed
to obtain a copy. So did British novelist William Harrison Ainsworth.
Having taken over editorship of *Bentley's Miscellany* from Dickens,
Ainsworth was on the prowl for good stories he could reprint in it.
He chose several from Poe's collection, starting with 'Why the Little
Frenchman Wears His Hand in a Sling', which he published in the July
1840 issue. This reprint scarcely helped Poe's reputation. Ainsworth
obfuscated his American source, publishing the story anonymously
and retitling it 'The Irish Gentleman and the Little Frenchman'.[1]

The London setting and Poe's humorous use of Irish brogue
to spoof British gentry made the tale appeal to English readers,
but Americans also enjoyed it. After its appearance in *Bentley's*,
William T. Porter reprinted the story in *Spirit of the Times*, the
New York sporting paper where some of the finest nineteenth-
century American literary humour appeared.[2] Though memorable
for its humour, 'Little Frenchman' is not without serious implica-
tions. It bears similarities to other tales and sketches Poe wrote as
the 1830s gave way to the following decade: 'The Philosophy of
Furniture', 'The Man of the Crowd' and 'The Murders in the Rue
Morgue'. All concern the theme of urban spectatorship in the
modern world, and each introduces a different type of spectator.

'The Man of the Crowd' prompted both Charles Baudelaire and Walter Benjamin to discuss the figure of the *flâneur*, the pedestrian who strolled the streets and arcades, observing the city and attempting to understand what he saw. By definition the *flâneur* takes the urban public space as both the location and the subject of his activities. Though the act of walking is typically associated with the *flâneur*, 'The Philosophy of Furniture' presents a paradoxical variant, the stationary *flâneur*.[3] This sketch takes the *flâneur* from the streets, puts him in the parlour, and has him take a good look around to see what he can and discern what it means.

The *badaud* or gawker emerged as an unsophisticated foil to the *flâneur*. In 'Enigmatical and Conundrum-ical', Poe had used this term in the following conundrum:

Why is the fifteenth letter of the alphabet, when mutilated,
    like a Parisian cockney?
Because it is a bad *O* – BADAUD.[4]

'The Philosophy of Furniture' introduces a *badaud*-like figure as a contrast to the narrator's *flâneur*-like observations. Arguing that the American fondness for decorative mirrors creates much interior ugliness, the narrator imagines how a *badaud* would react to a mirror-filled home: 'The veriest bumpkin, on entering an apartment so bedizzened, would be instantly aware of something wrong, although he might be altogether unable to assign a cause for his dissatisfaction.'[5]

Sir Patrick O'Grandison, the narrator of 'Little Frenchman', is also a bumpkin, as his rustic language clearly indicates.[6] Understood in terms of his visual sensibilities, he represents a more intrusive form of urban spectator. Whereas the narrator of 'The Philosophy of Furniture' restricts his gaze to the space of the private interior, Sir Patrick stares from his apartment into the private space of others' apartments. He is a voyeur, not a *flâneur*.

As of 1840, the term 'voyeur' had yet to enter English usage, so a synonym must suffice: Sir Patrick is a Peeping Tom. In Poe's *oeuvre*, the self-indulgent gaze of the *flâneur* and the Peeping Tom would ultimately achieve greater purpose with the inquisitive gaze of the detective in 'The Murders in the Rue Morgue'.

As Sir Patrick tells his tale, he looks from his window, sees the sling-wearing Frenchman in a neighbouring window, and explains the injury. Both men are suitors of the widow Mrs Treacle. They can see out of their respective windows into hers, and she can see out of hers into theirs. Sir Patrick's description of the Frenchman's behaviour – 'a oggling and a goggling the houl day' – also applies to his own behaviour. Convinced that the Frenchman's affections are misplaced, Sir Patrick is confident that he understands how Mrs Treacle feels. Reading her physical appearance and her gestures, he concludes that she loves him. Much of the humour of 'Little Frenchman' stems from the disparity between how the widow really feels about Sir Patrick and how he interprets her behaviour on the basis of what he sees.

'Little Frenchman' manifests its author's fascination with the possibility or, in Sir Patrick's case, impossibility of reading others on the basis of appearance. Poe had started exploring the legibility of external signs several years earlier. In 'Autography', for instance, he had reproduced autograph facsimiles from famous authors and attempted to discern their personalities on the basis of their handwriting. He further indulged the reading public's fascination with handwriting in a follow-up work, 'A Chapter on Autography', which drops the fictional pose of 'Autography' and bluntly explains how handwriting reflects individual personality. 'A Chapter on Autography' gave Poe a way to express subjective opinions while masking them in a guise of objectivity and letting him settle some personal scores in the process. The section on his previous employer, for example, reflects Poe's ongoing animosity toward his former boss. William Burton's 'scratchy and petite' handwriting reflects his 'indecision and care or caution'. Alternatively, Poe's positive remarks seem designed to curry favour. Louis Godey, whose magazine remained an important outlet for Poe, had 'remarkably distinct and graceful' handwriting: 'The man who invariably writes so well as Mr G. invariably does, gives evidence of a fine taste, combined with an indefatigability which will ensure his permanent success in the world's affairs.'[7]

The contemporary public's interest in handwriting reflects a general fascination with the way external signs could indicate personality. By the middle third of the nineteenth century, the whole world was becoming more legible – or so it seemed. Poe was writing in the era of phrenology, a time when self-proclaimed phrenologists travelled the country, charging people to feel the contours of their skulls and tell them who they were. Franz-Joseph Gall, a leading founder of phrenology, had mapped the skull, dividing it into different regions or organs, each representing a personal characteristic. Creativity and aesthetic appreciation, for example, were represented by the organ of ideality, located on the upper left forehead. George Combe, another founder of phrenology, observed:

Ideality delights in perfection from the pure pleasure of contemplating it. So far as it is concerned, the picture, the statue, the landscape, or the mansion, on which it abides with intensest rapture, will be as pleasing, although the property of another, as if all its own. It is a spring that is touched by the beautiful wherever it exists; and hence its means of enjoyment are as unbounded as the universe is extensive.[8]

Poe concurred. The term 'ideality' entered his critical vocabulary through the medium of phrenology, and the ideas it represented significantly influenced Poe's aesthetic theory. For instance, he called poet and travel writer Charles Fenno Hoffman 'a true idealist,

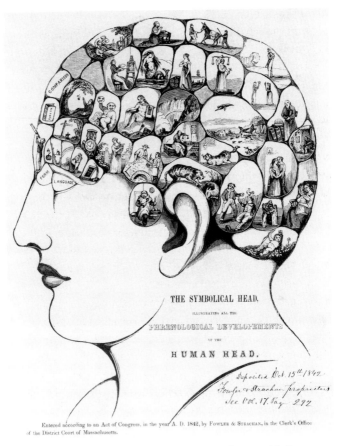

THE SYMBOLICAL HEAD,

ILLUSTRATING ALL THE

PHRENOLOGICAL DEVELOPEMENTS

OF THE

HUMAN HEAD.

Deposited Oct. 15th 1842.
Fowler & Strachan proprietors
See Vol. 17. Pag. 292

Entered according to an Act of Congress, in the year A. D. 1842, by FOWLER & STRACHAN, in the Clerk's Office of the District Court of Massachusetts.

The Symbolical Head: Illustrating All the Phrenological Developments of the Human Head, 1842.

in the proper phrenological sense' because he was 'sensitively alive to beauty in every development'.[9] According to the basic tenets of phrenology, great poets, being attuned to the beautiful, should naturally have giant foreheads.

Poe initially accepted phrenology as a valid science – mainly because it told him what he already knew. When F. W. Thomas asked him if he had ever had his head read, Poe replied, 'Speaking of heads – my own *has been* examined by several phrenologists – all of whom spoke of me in a species of extravaganza which I should be ashamed to repeat.'[10] Poe does not name his phrenologists, but one of them was Nelson Sizer, who criss-crossed the nation examining heads for forty years. Sizer came to Philadelphia when Poe lived there and gave him a phrenological reading. His enthusiastic interpretation confirms the extravagance Poe attributes to his phrenologists. Sizer exclaimed: 'How massive in the upper part of the forehead, in the region of Reasoning! How broad in the region of the temples, where Ideality, Constructiveness and Sublimity are located!'[11] Thomas Dunn English, who wrote his medical thesis on the relationship between phrenology and medicine, said of Poe: 'Ideality, with the power of analysis, is shown in his very broad, high and massive forehead – a forehead which would have delighted Gall beyond measure.'[12]

Roughly coeval with phrenology, photography contributed to the general feeling that the world was becoming more legible. Photographic portraits and engravings based on photographic images gave people the chance to phrenologize by proxy. They could pore over portraiture and understand the nature of those depicted by the shape of their heads. Poe clearly recognized the interrelationship of phrenology and photography. As a result, he was greatly disappointed with his first daguerreotype portrait: it did not properly display his prominent forehead. For subsequent daguerreotypes, Poe deliberately posed himself to show off his organ of ideality.[13] The strategy works. One phrenologist who judged him solely from his picture called his organ of ideality 'so large as to be almost a deformity in his personal appearance'.[14] Phrenology passed from vogue, but Poe's carefully crafted photographic image remains impressive. Indeed, his portraits have made his the most recognizable face in the history of American literature.

Poe made creative use of many other external signs that served to indicate personality. His first-person narrators often use the principles of physiognomy to read the personality of other characters on the basis of their facial features. Attire, physical gestures, gait, and posture provide additional ways to understand people. How others decorate their homes presents further clues for discerning identity. These different approaches toward understanding personality on the basis of external signs are all interrelated. Reading people's parlour furnishings is akin to reading their faces. Walter Benjamin made the parallel explicit. Speaking of 'The Philosophy of Furniture', he called Poe 'the first physiognomist of the domestic interior'.[15]

Appearing in late April 1840, 'The Philosophy of Furniture' was an occasional piece, meaning it was published for the occasion of Moving Day, 1 May, the day when annual leases expired and when New Yorkers who were going to move moved. Republishing 'The Philosophy of Furniture' five years later, Poe again timed its appearance to coincide with Moving Day. In this sketch Poe took the opportunity to describe the decor of the ideal room. To enhance his description, he placed an inhabitant inside: 'Even now, there is present to our mind's eye a small and not ostentatious chamber with whose decorations no fault can be found. The proprietor lies asleep on a sofa – the weather is cool – the time is near midnight: we will make a sketch of the room during his slumber.'[16] In other words, Poe catches the proprietor in the unconscious act of leaving his impression on the room as his body makes an indentation on the sofa. 'The Philosophy of Furniture', as Benjamin recognized, reflects the tendency of the nineteenth-century middle-class urban population to imprint themselves on their domestic environment. Poe's sketch verifies the close association between decor and personality and reinforces the identification between the character of a room and the personal character of its inhabitants. Depicting the home-owner asleep, Poe indicates that regardless of their level of conscious awareness, people continue to leave their mark on the spaces they inhabit.[17] He also blurs the boundary between the stationary *flâneur* and the Peeping Tom: there is a creepiness that comes with staring at someone asleep.

Through much of 1840, Poe worked hard to establish the *Penn Magazine*. He solicited subscriptions, lined up contributors and got the word out. Charles Alexander proved helpful. He puffed the proposed magazine in the *Daily Chronicle*, encouraging readers to subscribe. Despite Burton's fears, Poe's aggressive promotion did not prevent Burton from selling his magazine. In the third week of October, in fact, he sold *Burton's* to George R. Graham, publisher of *The Casket*, another literary monthly. Since Graham already owned a competing magazine, the principal benefit he received from purchasing *Burton's* was its list of subscribers. Graham paid Burton $3500, one dollar per subscriber. Graham did not intend to continue *Burton's*. Instead, he would combine it with *The Casket* to form *Graham's Magazine*.

Poe's hard work toward establishing the *Penn Magazine* was bringing the project closer to reality, but it was not putting any bread on the table. Since his dismissal, the covers of *Burton's* had been closed to him for the most part. Upon taking over the magazine, Graham welcomed Poe's work. Its last issue, simultaneously the last issue of *The Casket* and a sample issue of the forthcoming *Graham's Magazine*, contained 'The Man of the Crowd', which deserves recognition as one of Poe's major tales. The issue hit news-stands in late November 1840.

'The Man of the Crowd' also takes the legibility of the modern world as its theme. As Poe's narrator relates his London experience, he describes himself seated in the bow window of a London coffee-house, alternately reading a newspaper and observing his surroundings. These two parallel activities make the act of observing analogous to the reading process.[18] Every face in the crowd becomes a text for the narrator to read. He takes pride in his ability to discern personality on the basis of external appearance:

'Although the rapidity with which the world of life flitted before the window, prevented me from casting more than a glance upon each visage, still it seemed that in my peculiar mental state, I could frequently read, even in that brief interval of a glance, the history of long years.'[19] Revising 'The Man of the Crowd' for republication, Poe made several brief changes to enhance its complexity. For one, he altered the phrase 'world of life' to 'world of light', suggesting that we do not see people as they really are: we only see what their exteriors reflect. We see the light, not the life. Unable to identify a mysterious old man who enters his visual field, the narrator leaves the comfort of the coffee-house and heads into the street in pursuit. He follows the old man through the London streets all night, commenting on the appearance of the city as he goes.

In terms of literary antecedents, 'The Man of the Crowd' closely resembles the city sketch, a minor literary genre that describes the life of a city, typically starting at daybreak, continuing through the day and extending into the night. Princess Marie Bonaparte called 'The Man of the Crowd' a 'symphony in "ebony and silver" of the lamp-lit night of a great city'.[20] Her words reinforce the association between 'The Man of the Crowd' and the city sketch and also link Poe's tale with a landmark work in motion picture history, Walter Ruttman's *Berlin, Symphony of a Great City*, a grand cinematic version of the city sketch. Furthermore, Bonaparte's words associate Poe's story with photography. Like the daguerreotype portrait, whose invention was made public the year before, Poe's tale attempts to capture man's identity. In terms of the history of photography, 'The Man of the Crowd' resembles no other work more closely than the photography of Lisette Model, whose most memorable images depict people in a fragmented and depersonalized way. She portrays men's lower legs and feet as they hurry through the modern city streets. Like the old man of Poe's tale, her subjects are men of the crowd, men who remain fragmented, whose precise identities remain elusive.

Despite his lengthy pursuit, the narrator gets no closer to understanding the man he follows. He concludes that the old man is 'the type and the genius of deep crime. He refuses to be alone. *He is the man of the crowd.*'[21] The narrator's conclusion reflects paranoia bred from uncertainty. Back in the coffeehouse, he had been absolutely confident in his ability to read the faces in the crowd. Now, after a night on the streets, his confidence is shattered. His inability to read the old man frightens him. Few experiences are more terrifying than encountering the unreadable in a world we thought we could read, the unknown in a world we thought we knew.

Though one tale is serious and the other humorous, the action of 'The Man of the Crowd' parallels the action of 'Little Frenchman'. Once the Frenchman visits Sir Patrick and tells him that he, too, loves Mrs Treacle, Sir Patrick must follow him to her apartment to keep him under surveillance. In other words, he must leave the safety of his own private space and venture into the dangerous space of the widow's apartment, where he can no longer control what will happen. The two men woo, but, caring for neither, she has her footmen throw them out. Poe lets Sir Patrick return home to his apartment, where he looks out his window once more and reconstructs his fantasy. The narrator of 'The Man of the Crowd' leaves his cosy coffee-house for much the same reason Sir Patrick leaves his comfortable apartment: for the purpose of surveillance. Unlike Sir Patrick, the narrator never returns to where he started. Nor does he recapture his smug certainty. The action of the story ends with him standing by himself on an empty London street, his pursuit ended, his quest thwarted. The individual alone in a big city and unable to comprehend his fellow man: with this image, Poe painted the portrait of modern man.

Around the time 'The Man of the Crowd' appeared, Poe trekked to Andalusia, the country estate of Nicholas Biddle. Best known as the president of the Second Bank of the United States, Biddle was now retired. Poe did not know him personally, but the two had much in common. Biddle was a literary man and a patron of the arts and sciences; his home was becoming a salon visited by European and American litterateurs.[22] Earlier he had helped edit *History of the Expedition under the Command of Captains Lewis and Clark*, a significant source for 'The Journal of Julius Rodman' and a major work of American literature in its own right. Biddle was also a correspondent of Poe's kinsman George Poe, Jr, an Alabama banker to whom Poe also appealed for support. He found Biddle affable and greatly enjoyed discussing English literature with him.[23]

The precise nature of his visit to Andalusia is uncertain, but it had something to do with the *Penn Magazine*. Discussing the magazine a few months earlier, Poe had expressed his desire to form a connection 'with some gentleman of literary attainments, who could at the same time advance as much ready money as will be requisite for the first steps of the undertaking'.[24] Biddle qualified in terms of both literary attainments and ready money.

Andalusia, Bucks County, Pennsylvania, south elevation, showing hexastyle doric portico.

To ingratiate himself, Poe presented him an autographed copy of *Tales of the Grotesque and Arabesque*. Poe's sales pitch left Biddle unconvinced. He hesitated to invest but agreed to a four-year subscription, which was a kind of patronage. Biddle understood that new magazines seldom lasted that long.

Shortly after returning from Andalusia, Poe was stricken ill and confined to bed for around a month. Consequently, he had to delay his plans for the *Penn Magazine*, the first number of which he had hoped to issue in January 1841. March was his new goal. In the first week of January he wrote Biddle to inform him of the delay but also to ask another favour. Poe hoped he would contribute an article to the magazine's first issue:

> Without friends in Philadelphia, except among literary men as uninfluential as myself, I would at once be put in a good position – I mean in respect to that all important point, caste – by having it known that you were not indifferent to my success. You will not accuse me of intending the meanness of flattery to serve as a selfish purpose, when I say that your name has an almost illimitable influence in the city, and a vast influence in all quarters of the country.[25]

Making this request, Poe could not fully mask his melancholy. As hard as he had worked to make a name for himself as an author, the name of a banker still meant more to the American public.

Poe continued soliciting subscriptions and lining up contributors, but when a nationwide financial crisis struck the first week of February, he was forced to postpone plans for the *Penn Magazine* indefinitely – a prudent decision, according to George Graham. 'Periodicals are among the principal sufferers by these pecuniary convulsions,' Graham observed, 'and to *commence* one just now would be exceedingly hazardous.'[26] Sensitive to Poe's disappointment, Graham asked him to take charge of the book review department of *Graham's Magazine,* offering an annual salary of eight hundred dollars. The salary was better than any Poe had yet received or, for that matter, better than any salary he ever would receive. What made the opportunity most appealing to Poe was the intellectual freedom Graham offered. Whereas Burton had severely restricted what Poe could say in his reviews, Graham would give him the freedom to express his mind. Poe accepted.

The April 1841 issue of *Graham's* announced Poe's association with the magazine on its front cover: 'Mr Poe is too well known in the literary world to require a word of commendation. As a critic he is surpassed by no man in this country; and as in this Magazine his critical abilities shall have free scope, the rod will be very generously, and at the same time, justly administered.'[27] This issue also contained Poe's review of Edward Bulwer-Lytton's *Night and Morning* and another major tale, 'The Murders in the Rue Morgue'.

The sheer length of Poe's review of *Night and Morning* indicates an important difference between *Burton's* and *Graham's.* The review of this novel is five and a half pages long, each page consisting of two columns of closely printed text. It begins with a plot summary, but even as Poe sketches out the plot, his words reflect concerns similar to those of current tales. Robert Beaufort, one of the novel's principal characters, Poe calls 'a crafty man-of-the-world, whose only honesty consists in appearing honest – a scrupulous decorist'.[28]

Here Poe broadens the meaning of the word 'decorist'. And why not? He coined it. The earliest known usage of the word occurs seven years earlier in 'The Visionary', in which it means someone who takes a superficial attitude toward interior design. Poe's review of *Night and Morning* adds a further nuance, suggesting the same word could be applied to personal appearance as well as home decor. People who are decorists create superficial personal appearances that do not necessarily reflect their personalities. The double meaning of the word 'decorist' reinforces the parallel between physiognomy and interior decor.

Poe coined many other words. Understanding that neologisms could revitalize the language and develop its expressive powers, he never hesitated to invent words whenever necessary. According to the *Oxford English Dictionary*, other words Poe added to the English language include: belaud, bemirror, bullyism, circumgyratory, disenchain, elocutionary, elocutionize, Macauleyism, markedness, melodramatism, mispunctuate, multicolour, mystific, normality, overscore, paragraphism, pesty, phaseless, quotability, scoriae, sentience, Shelleyan, spasmodist, spherify, tintinnabulation, unanswerability, unclassifiable, unindividualized, unmined, unmouldered, and many, many more.

In his critical work, Poe sought to define literary terms more precisely. In the review of *Night and Morning*, for instance, he specifically defines the word 'plot': 'that in which no part can be displaced without ruin to the whole.'[29] This definition helps explain the meticulous craftsmanship he brought to his own fiction. Coleridge said that in a poem every word counts. Poe went one better. Not only does every word count, but the *position* of each word also counts. Furthermore, this rigorous aesthetic applies to prose as well as verse. Few works better exemplify Poe's definition of plot than 'The Murders in the Rue Morgue'.

Widely recognized as the first detective story in literary history, 'The Murders in the Rue Morgue' established the conventions of the genre. The tale is narrated by the comparatively slow-witted friend of master sleuth C. Auguste Dupin. Together the two men visit a crime scene to unravel the mystery of how two women were murdered inside a locked apartment. Arthur Conan Doyle's Sherlock Holmes is a direct descendant of C. Auguste Dupin, and Dr Watson bears an uncanny resemblance to Poe's narrator. Agatha Christie owes a debt to Poe as well. Hercule Poirot directly descends from Dupin, and Colonel Hastings follows Poe's narrator. Rex Stout's Nero Wolfe and his assistant Archie Goodwin also resemble Dupin and Poe's narrator.

Poe brought Dupin back for two sequels: 'The Mystery of Marie Rogêt' and 'The Purloined Letter'. Based on a true story, 'Marie Rogêt' retells the story of the mysterious death of Mary Rogers, a New York cigar girl who perished from a botched abortion. Poe changed her name and relocated the story to Paris, but contemporary readers easily recognized his inspiration. 'The Purloined Letter', a more effective tale, tells the story of a stolen letter the prefect of police cannot locate. The bumbling police detective is another convention of the detective story Poe introduced. Dupin, on the other hand, is able to locate the letter because he possesses the imagination the police lack. The ideal detective, like the ideal poet, has both reason and imagination.

In 'The Murders in the Rue Morgue', Dupin solves the mystery by asking a fundamental question. As he tells the narrator, 'In investigations such as we are now pursuing, it should not be so much asked "what has occurred", as "what has occurred that has never occurred before".'[30] Dupin applies his question to solve a crime; Guy Debord has since recognized that the same question can be applied to plumb the mysteries of modern existence.[31] Poe may have isolated the anonymous individual in 'The Man of the Crowd', but the figure of Dupin offers man an escape or, at least, a way toward understanding. By discerning what occurs now that has never occurred before, man can find a path to truth and, possibly, a means of coping with the uncertainties of modern life.

Editing Poe's short stories, Thomas O. Mabbott placed 'Why the Little Frenchman Wears His Hand in a Sling' at the end of one major period of fiction and 'The Murders in the Rue Morgue' at the start of the next major period. In between he placed a short section of tales including 'The Philosophy of Furniture' and 'The Man of the Crowd'. Labelling this section 'Interlude', Mabbott inadvertently revealed that he did not quite know what to do with the works that fell within this brief period. But there is a continuity that extends from the end of one major period to the start of the next across this so-called interlude. All these tales take for their subject the legibility of the modern world. The differences among them depend upon who is doing the reading.

Sir Patrick, the bumpkin-like Peeping Tom, gets himself in trouble with Mrs Treacle because he misunderstands her behaviour. He projects his feelings onto her, and she reflects back his desire, which he misinterprets as hers. The *flâneur*-like narrators of 'The Philosophy of Furniture' and 'The Man of the Crowd' have considerable ability to read others, though one has a significant advantage. The narrator of 'The Philosophy of Furniture' watches an inhabitant imprinting himself onto the physical space of his living room, whereas the narrator of 'The Man of the Crowd' must interpret those he sees on the fly. His initial confidence disappears as he realizes the limitations of his ability to read others. Dupin combines the abilities of both. He can interpret the physical space of the crime scene, but he can also read others' thoughts as they walk silently through the night-time streets.

The underlying reason for Dupin's profound detective abilities remains uncertain in 'The Murders in the Rue Morgue' and 'The Mystery of Marie Rogêt', but in 'The Purloined Letter' Poe reveals why Dupin is such a good detective. When the prefect of police scoffs at the idea of being a poet, Dupin humbly admits that he has been 'guilty of certain doggerel' himself.[32] In other words, Dupin is a poet as well as a detective. He personally combines the powers of reason and imagination, each of which enhances the other. In the detective process, reason can take the detective only so far. Assembling the facts and making all the necessary deductions initiates the detective process, but to solve a crime properly, the detective must make an imaginative leap. Viewing a crime scene, the man of reason sees what is, but the poet is the one who imagines what has happened.

6

The Tourist's Gaze

Poe continued doing good work for *Graham's Magazine*. 'A Descent into the Maelström', a thrilling tale of life-threatening danger, appeared in the May 1841 issue. Structured as a frame tale, this story marks another advance in Poe's narrative technique. Beginning in the voice of an outside narrator – an American tourist – the narrative gives way to an old sailor who has experienced first-hand the harrowing dangers of the famous whirlpool off the coast of Norway. In a structural variation, the outside narrator never returns to finish the story; the inside narrator gets the last word. 'A Descent into the Maelström' explores another new type of person who, like the businessman and the detective, was coming to define the modern world: the tourist.

The word 'tourist' had entered the English language in the late eighteenth century, but its meaning shifted in the early nineteenth. Initially synonymous with 'traveller', it slowly gathered negative connotations.[1] Poe's work tracks the shift. In 1840 he called his trailblazing explorer Julius Rodman a 'tourist', but three years later he saw the tourist as a dandy in silk stockings. Discussing Charles Fenno Hoffman's *Winter in the West* three more years later, Poe observed: 'Its scenic descriptions are vivid, because fresh, genuine, unforced. There is nothing of the cant of the tourist for the sake not of nature but of *tourism*.'[2] During the half dozen years separating the Rodman story and the Hoffman article, Poe portrayed the tourist in several short stories, questioning the kind of leisure they symbolized.

Before coming to Norway, the outside narrator of 'A Descent into the Maelström' had seen America first. Admitting to, even boasting about his familiarity with Niagara Falls, he clearly identifies himself as a tourist. By 1841 the world-famous falls attracted thousands of visitors annually. One contemporary observer called Niagara Falls 'the great magnet of the tourist'.[3] The narrator has also visited the American prairies, a destination for tourists with the time, cash, and patience to make the trip. Poe would link both destinations together under the general category of 'natural lions of the land'.[4] The outside narrator's trip to Norway seems similarly motivated. He has come to see another geographical lion: the Norway maelstrom.

Whereas the outside narrator's travel constitutes a leisure activity, the inside narrator travels as part of his work. As the old fisherman explains why he and his brothers risked the maelstrom's dangers, his words echo early American promotion literature. 'In all violent eddies at sea there is good fishing, at proper opportunities, if one has only the courage to attempt it', he explains. 'In fact, we made it a matter of desperate speculation – the risk of life standing instead of labor, and courage answering for capital.'[5] Like early American settlers, the fisherman was willing to endanger his life for the sake of his livelihood.

The old man leads the tourist to a lofty precipice overlooking the famous whirlpool, where he explains that his frightening encounter with the maelstrom had completely unnerved him. He asks, 'Do you know I can scarcely look over this little cliff without getting giddy?'[6] The tourist identifies a disparity between what the old man says and how he acts:

The 'little cliff', upon whose edge he had so carelessly thrown himself down to rest that the weightier portion of his body hung over it, while he was only kept from falling by the tenure of his elbow on its extreme and slippery edge – this 'little cliff' arose, a sheer unobstructed precipice of black shining rock, some fifteen or sixteen hundred feet from the world of crags beneath us. Nothing would have tempted me to within half a dozen yards of its brink. In truth so deeply was I excited by the perilous position of my companion, that I fell at full length upon the ground, clung to the shrubs around me, and dared not even glance upward at the sky – while I struggled in vain to divest myself of the idea that the very foundations of the mountain were in danger from the fury of the winds. It was long before I could reason myself into sufficient courage to sit up and look out into the distance.[7]

With these words Poe belittles the tourist in contrast to his guide. 'A Descent into the Maelström' celebrates the working man. Having risked his life to make a living, the sailor has undergone a metamorphosis. He says that the experience broke him, but he has really emerged with a new attitude toward danger. Unlike the tourist, the old fisherman thinks nothing of perching himself on the precarious edge of the cliff. The tourist, alternatively, is solely a sightseer. He comes to see something dangerous but has no wish to put himself in harm's way. He wants risk-free sightseeing.

The contrast between the fisherman and tourist – work and leisure – captures one of the major tensions in Poe's life. As a young man he had imagined being a gentleman of independent means with sufficient leisure to write poetry without having to worry how to make a living. Many of his literary friends were professional men, physicians and lawyers, for whom writing was a leisure activity. Since John Allan's death, literature had been Poe's livelihood, pitiful as it was. Poe identified with the old man in 'A Descent into the Maelström'. He, too, encountered the sublime as part of his work. He, too, put himself – his health and his sanity – at risk for the sake of his livelihood.

'The Island of the Fay', a sketch that appeared in the next issue of *Graham's*, can be read as a companion piece to 'A Descent into the

Maelström'. With the development of tourism, major attractions became more and more important. These extraordinary destinations gave people a way to separate themselves from everyday experience and subsequently served as markers of status.[8] Dropping the names of holiday destinations became akin to social namedropping. 'The Island of the Fay' implicitly questions the value of the major attraction. A natural setting need be neither sublime nor spectacular nor even famous to create a worthwhile natural experience. By venturing into some nearby woods alone, a person can enjoy nature fully. 'The Island of the Fay' celebrates the imaginative possibilities that come with the contemplation of natural scenery.

After some general comments on the aesthetic appreciation of nature, this sketch relates an afternoon in the life of its narrator. Enjoying the scenery, he watches the trees cast shadows across a nearby stream. The lengthening shadows create weird visual effects, letting him imagine a fairy encircling an islet in the stream. Though Poe enjoyed rambling through the wooded areas around Philadelphia, 'The Island of the Fay' is not based on personal experience. Technically, it is a plate article. Graham assigned him the task of writing text to accompany a fanciful engraving he planned to publish.

Plate articles suited Poe's compositional process. As he explained in his *Graham's* review of Nathaniel Hawthorne's *Twice Told Tales* the following year, an author imagines a single effect for a work, then creates incidents to achieve that effect. A plate article essentially imposed an ultimate effect, but it did give Poe the freedom to imagine incidents leading to it. Though 'The Island of the Fay' was based on a visual image instead of a natural scene, the actual source mattered little to Poe. The contemplation of art, like the contemplation of nature, could fire his imagination.

Poe used a painting as a motif in another tourist tale he published in *Graham's*, 'Life in Death', better known in revised form as 'The Oval Portrait'. Though Niagara Falls attracted many tourists in Poe's day, the social elite remained strongly attached to Italy and the Mediterranean. Taking his narrator to the Apennines in 'The Oval Portrait', Poe marked him as a tourist. The 'mass of English', according to a contemporary, 'swarmed over the Continent, century after century, trampling the snows of Alps and Apennines'.[9] Such diction portrays tourists as pests. 'The Oval Portrait' presents a

Alfred Kubin, *The Oval Portrait*, reprinted from *Hans Pfaalls Mondreise und Andere Novellen*.

similar impression. Encountering a vacant chateau, the narrator breaks down the door and stays the night. His behaviour suggests that the picturesque exists for the tourist's consumption.

The narrator retires to a bedroom filled with paintings. Settling himself in bed, he reads for awhile, pausing at one point to adjust the candles. Repositioned, they illuminate a painting of a beautiful woman. He spends time contemplating the portrait but ultimately readjusts the light to cast the painting in shadow. He then picks up a nearby guidebook, which explains that the sitter died just as the artist finished the painting.

Like 'A Descent into the Maelström', 'The Oval Portrait' is a frame tale without a closing frame. The guidebook text forms the inside narration and ends the tale. This structure has much the same effect in both stories. Traditionally, travellers hired guides, but Baedekers and other guidebooks had recently emerged to suit the growing number of European tourists.[10] Giving one of his tourist-narrators a personal guide and another a written one, Poe suggested that there was essentially no difference between the two. In both cases, tourists let others interpret for them. Sightseeing prevents them from sight-imagining. The tourist in 'A Descent into the Maelström' sacrifices his imagination as he lets the old fisherman tell the story. Instead of contemplating the portrait and letting it take his imagination where it will, the narrator of 'The Oval Portrait' deliberately cloaks it in shadow.

In April 1842, the same month 'Life in Death' appeared, Poe resigned from *Graham's* disgusted 'with the namby-pamby character of the Magazine': the 'contemptible pictures, fashion-plates, music and love tales'.[11] Poe also felt unappreciated. *Graham's* flourished during his tenure with the magazine, but Poe received little remuneration or recognition for the magazine's burgeoning success. He and Graham parted on amicable terms; Poe would keep contributing to the magazine. In retrospect his decision to quit seems impulsive and ill-considered. He may not have liked the magazine's general character, but Graham had given him a regular salary, the freedom to voice his critical opinions and encouragement to publish groundbreaking tales.

Poe's fascination with the tourist may be the most consistent thread running though his tales of the early 1840s, but he experimented with other themes. 'The Colloquy of Monos and Una' presents a celestial dialogue between two lovers reunited after death who lament the state of civilization. 'Never Bet the Devil Your Head' satirizes the nascent cult of celebrity, as Federico Fellini realized when he updated the tale for the cinema as 'Toby Dammit'. 'Eleonora', a love story inspired by Bernardin de Saint-Pierre's *Paul et Virginie*, captured the attention of contemporary readers and was widely reprinted in the US and the UK. The *Great Western Magazine*, to take an unrecorded London reprint for example, included 'Eleonora' in its April 1842 issue.[12] And 'The Masque of the Red Death' is a *tour de force*, complex in its visual imagery and symbolic resonance.

Graham hired Rufus Griswold to succeed Poe. Having worked a series of minor editorial positions in New England, Griswold established his reputation with *The Poets and Poetry of America*, which brought him to Graham's attention. Poe had met Griswold in Philadelphia the previous year, when they 'had a long conversation about literature and literary men'.[13] After reading *The Poets and Poetry of America*, Jesse Dow sized up Griswold and found him wanting. Hearing Griswold had replaced Poe, Dow editorialized, 'We would give more for Edgar A. Poe's toe nail, than we would for Rueful Grizzle's soul, unless we wanted a milk-strainer. Them's our sentiments.'[14]

Out of work Poe had to hustle to survive. He began preparing a multi-volume collected edition of his tales, to be called *Phantasy-Pieces*. His devotion to his *oeuvre* is admirable, but his plans show surprisingly little awareness of the literary marketplace. Book-buyers were no more anxious to buy collections of previously published short stories now than they had been the previous decade. They were even more reluctant to buy expensive multi-volume collections.

A manuscript note on the proposed table of contents instructs the printer to preserve the order of the listed stories. Poe obviously devoted much thought to his organization, though an organizational scheme is not readily apparent. The placement of 'The Conversation of Eiros and Charmion' as the final story makes sense. An apocalyptic tale depicting events leading to earth's destruction by a comet, this story would make the end of the world and the end of the book coterminous, transforming the entire collection into an apocalypic vision. Other aspects of Poe's organization are difficult to discern. Twenty-nine tales separate 'The Murders in the Rue Morgue', the first work listed, from its sequel, 'The Mystery of Marie Rogêt'. Poe obviously did not want to clump together his detective stories. But how did he organize the collection?

His principles of organization anticipate the thought of Sergei Eisenstein. Montage, the primary idea underlying Eisenstein's cinematic work, occurs when a new concept arises from the juxta-position of two separate texts. In Poe's table of contents, 'Lionizing' directly follows 'A Descent into the Maelström'. This juxtaposition encourages readers to compare how people react to the 'natural lions of the land' and how they react to the lions of society. Im-plicitly, those who lionize celebrities are no different from the bug-eyed tourists who gawk at Niagara Falls with mouths agape. Poe organized his tales to give readers new ways of seeing, to see beyond the texts of individual stories and recognize the connec-tions between them.

In the fourth week of June 1842 Poe left Philadelphia for New York, where he hoped to find a publisher for *Phantasy-Pieces* and a position with one of the city's magazines. He had at least two magazines in mind, the *Ladies' Companion* and the *Democratic Review*. That Poe even considered approaching William Snowden's namby-pamby

Ladies' Companion suggests he was having second thoughts about leaving *Graham's*. The *Democratic Review*, alternatively, was a respected monthly published by James and Henry G. Langley. An editorial position on it could catapult Poe to the top of his profession.

Before seeing the Langleys, Poe ran into William Ross Wallace, a Kentucky native hoping to establish himself as a New York poet. Poe originally met him in Philadelphia, where Wallace spent time lollygagging around the *Graham's* office.[15] The two became friends and sometimes read their unpublished work to each other. Another friend called Wallace 'a delightful companion to meet if you met him at the right time'.[16] In a congenial mood when they met in New York, Wallace invited Poe for a mint julep. Beyond the watchful eyes of his wife and mother-in-law, Poe was more susceptible to such invitations. Typically served in a large bar glass with 'a coquettish forest of mint' sprouting from its top, the julep was well-nigh irresistible. Charles Fenno Hoffman called it 'the drink of immortals'.[17]

The two men apparently met in the late morning. As a somewhat astonished British visitor to New York commented, 'The eleven-o'clock-in-the-morning julep with the lunch of the *café* is a received fact.'[18] Wallace and Poe finished their juleps with plenty of time left in the business day. In a drink-induced lapse in judgement, Poe called on Robert Hamilton, associate editor of the *Ladies' Companion.* This same afternoon he also met the Langleys. Poe's visit to them is known because of his subsequent letter of apology in which he admitted, 'I knew not what I was either doing or saying.'[19] Needless to say, he did not get the job. This drinking spree continued beyond the bounds of Manhattan. Mary Starr, now married and living in Jersey City, remembered Poe crossing the ferry into New Jersey to see her. (Getting drunk and looking up old girlfriends is not a recent phenomenon.) After a brief stay, Eddie, as Mary told the story, ended up in the woods outside Jersey City, 'wandering about like a crazy man'.[20]

Poe was not so embarrassed by his behaviour that he stopped seeking the Langleys' help. In the third week of July he sent them his latest tale, 'The Landscape Garden'. They politely returned it. Undaunted, he next sent it to the more open-minded Hamilton, who accepted it for the *Ladies' Companion*, allowing Poe five dollars for the story. It appeared in October 1842. With this tale Poe continued exploring the relationship between the tourist and the lions of the land. If tourists insist on visiting famous sites of natural beauty, Poe suggested, then let's not leave what they see solely to chance. 'The Landscape Garden' imagines the possibility of creating a major natural attraction. The story essentially asks the question: given unlimited funds and time, could someone create the most beautiful landscape ever, a landscape more beautiful than any nature created?

The question intrigued Poe, and he returned to it five years later when he revised 'The Landscape Garden' into 'The Domain of Arnheim'. Whereas the earlier story presents the theory underlying the creation of an ideal landscape, the later one details precisely what a visit to that landscape would be like. Transforming one story into another, Poe was partly influenced by J. D. Harding's *Principles and Practice of Art*, a copy of which passed through his hands around 1845.[21] Harding – John Ruskin's drawing master – argued that art should celebrate the infinite variety of nature and that the spectator should be an active participant in aesthetic appreciation. 'The Domain of Arnheim' incorporates both ideas.

A boat takes the visitor to the middle of a lake, where he or she transfers to a canoe: 'On its ermined floor reposes a single feathery paddle of satin-wood; but no oarsman or attendant is to be seen. The guest is bidden to be of good cheer – that the fates will take care of him.'[22] Poe was speaking figuratively, of course. The Fates were not the ones moving that canoe. Poe did not explain precisely how it moved, but apparently a huge mechanical apparatus akin to an underwater railway track propelled it. Providing visitors with such an extravagant ride, Poe foresaw the modern-day theme park.[23] But the theme to Poe's proto-Disneyland is not popular amusement, but aesthetic pleasure. Visitors to Arnheimland enter an immense work of art.

The lavish descriptions in 'The Landscape Garden' and 'The Domain of Arnheim' show that Poe did not let his dire circumstances restrain his imagination. His ability to transcend personal squalor to create timeless works of art may be the most remarkable aspect of his life. Borges thought so. 'Poe taught me how to use my imagination', Borges admitted. 'He taught me – though I was unaware of it, but I must have felt it strongly – that one may not be tied down by mere everyday circumstances: that being tied down to everyday circumstances stood for poverty, stood for dullness. I could be everywhere, and I could be, let's say, in eternity. And I suppose Poe taught me that. He taught me the width, the vastness of freedom.'[24]

To supplement the meagre income he received from his tales, Poe also sought outlets for his critical work. Around the time he went to New York in July 1842, Griswold asked him to review *The Poets and Poetry of America*, promising to find a magazine that would accept the review and offering to pay Poe ahead of time. Griswold was essentially bribing him for a positive notice. Grateful for the money, Poe nonetheless refused to compromise his critical standards. He critiqued what needed to be critiqued, especially Griswold's overt New England bias. Despite his criticism, Poe's review was generally quite positive. He said Griswold had written *The Poets and Poetry of America* with judgment, dignity, and candour.[25] In light of his negative comments, Poe was sure Griswold would not publish the review. Griswold did think Poe could have been more generous in his praise, but he did not suppress the review. He had promised to publish it, and he did. Griswold sent it to the *Boston Miscellany*, which slated the review for its November issue.

Before the summer of 1842 ended, Poe moved his family to a small row house on Coates Street in the Fairmount district of Philadelphia. Maria Clemm kept the house 'neat and orderly', but even she could not mask the 'air of pecuniary want'.[26] Located on the edge of town, their new home was close to the Wissahickon River, or Wissahiccon, as Poe spelled it. He enjoyed walking through the woods along the river. Beyond the opportunities for contemplation, the river also gave Poe opportunities for sport and sustenance. His military training had made Poe a crack shot. The boy next door remembered, 'When Poe asked me to go with him for reed birds I went. I was an active boy. We got into a boat and paddled down to about Gray's Ferry. I rowed while he loaded and shot. For many of the birds I waded in water up to my chin. We brought home a big bag.'[27]

Mostly Poe kept busy with piecemeal literary work. *The Gift for 1843* accepted 'The Pit and the Pendulum', a graphic story of medieval torture subtly structured as a dream vision, which a contemporary reader called 'one of his sombre and thrilling narratives, exhibiting the intense nature of his "graver musings"'.[28] *Graham's* accepted the retrospective review of Rufus Dawes that Burton had rejected years earlier. And Snowden accepted 'The Mystery of Marie Rogêt', publishing it in three instalments in the *Ladies' Companion.* But all this scattered work frustrated Poe. He longed for a magazine of his own.

He was not alone. Several of his ambitious literary friends dreamed the same dream – and experienced similar frustrations. After establishing the semi-weekly Washington *Index* in August 1841, Jesse Dow kept it afloat as long as he could. The *Index* initially proved successful, going from semi-weekly to tri-weekly to daily over its first year, but the endeavour nearly exhausted the otherwise energetic Dow. Suffering from illness in July 1842, he resigned as editor. Without Dow's leadership, the paper languished. The *Index* instantly reverted to a tri-weekly and folded a month later.

James Russell Lowell, *c.* 1860.

Also this year James Russell Lowell planned his own magazine, *The Pioneer*. He accepted 'The Tell-Tale Heart' for his first issue, which appeared in January 1843. The way Lowell paid Poe indicates the tenuous financing of contemporary periodicals. At the moment Lowell did not have sufficient funds to pay for Poe's contribution to *The Pioneer*. Meanwhile Graham still owed Lowell money for a contribution to his magazine. Consequently Lowell asked Graham to pay Poe out of what he (Graham) owed him (Lowell). Eager to cultivate his relationship with *The Pioneer*, Poe offered to write a new article for each issue. Lowell agreed. After the third issue, however, Lowell found himself hopelessly in debt and suffering from a debilitating eye injury that required surgery to save his sight. There was no fourth issue of *The Pioneer*.

In the second week of December 1842, Philadelphia publisher Thomas Cottrell Clarke issued the first number of his mammoth weekly, the *Philadelphia Saturday Museum*. Poe's precise involvement with this paper is unclear, yet he sufficiently befriended its proprietor that Clarke agreed to publish Poe's long-planned magazine, now called *The Stylus*. To promote the magazine, which they hoped to launch the first half of 1843, Clarke decided to include some advance publicity in the *Saturday Museum*. The 25 February 1843 issue was covered with all things Poe. His prospectus appeared on the back page, and the front page contained Henry Hirst's biography of Poe accompanied by a wood-engraved portrait based on a recent daguerreotype, which was reprinted the following week. Such publicity was just what Poe needed to promote his new magazine.

The second week of March 1843 brought Poe to Washington – the 'land of excitement and rascality', as F. W. Thomas called it.[29] Since obtaining a clerkship with the Treasury Department, Thomas had held out the possibility that Poe could obtain some kind of clerical position with the Tyler administration and thus free himself from relying on his pen to survive. Later that year Dow, who also lived in Washington, would be elected Doorkeeper of the House of Representatives, a position bringing him a $1500 salary and giving him time to write. The possibility of employment in Washington for Poe had faded, but he hoped for a place with the Collector of Customs in Philadelphia. Coming to Washington, he planned to see Robert Tyler, the president's son, to assure his appointment with US Customs. He also hoped to generate further support for *The Stylus*.

The story of Poe's trip to Washington is almost predictable. He checked in at Fuller's City Hotel at Pennsylvania Avenue and Fourteenth Street, where Thomas roomed. But Thomas was ill, so Poe had to fend for himself. The hotel bar lured him inside, where a glass of port initiated another lengthy drinking spree. The extent of his drunken behaviour has gone unrecorded. Dow mentioned some 'senseless creatures' making sport at Poe's expense, and Poe admitted walking around with his coat inside out at one point and generally making a fool of himself at Fuller's Hotel.[30] His old nemesis John Hill Hewitt, who now lived in Washington, met him on Pennsylvania Avenue one day. 'Seedy in appearance and woebegone', Poe shook his hand and asked him to forget the past. Hewitt recalled, 'He said he had not had a mouthful of food since the day previous, and begged me to lend him fifty cents to obtain a meal. Though he looked the used-up man all over – still he showed the gentleman. I gave him the money.'[31]

Dow grew so concerned about Poe's wayward behaviour that he wrote to Clarke, asking him to come and retrieve him. Dow could safely get Poe on the train but worried that he would get off at Baltimore and continue his spree there. Clarke, a temperance man, did not like hearing such news, especially about a possible business partner. His relationship with Poe briefly remained cordial, but before another two months had passed, Clarke withdrew his financial support for *The Stylus*. Once again Poe had to abandon his planned magazine.

Edgar Allan Poe House, 530 North Seventh Street (rear), Philadelphia.

Despite his personal failings, Poe was determined to succeed as an author. In or before March 1843 he completed 'The Gold Bug' and submitted it to Graham, who accepted it, magnanimously paying Poe fifty-two dollars, money that allowed him and his family to rent a house on Seventh Street in the Spring Garden district just north of Philadelphia. When the Philadelphia *Dollar Magazine* advertised a literary contest with a hundred-dollar first prize, Poe thought 'The Gold Bug' would make an ideal submission and asked for the story back. Graham agreed and, even more magnanimously, let Poe repay the fifty-two dollars not in cash but in additional articles for *Graham's*. On Wednesday, 14 June, the *Dollar Newspaper* announced the winner of the hundred-dollar grand prize: 'The Gold Bug'. Illustrated by F.O.C. Darley, the story appeared over the next two weeks. Poe's most successful tale to date, 'The Gold Bug' was reprinted across the USA, dramatized for the American stage, translated into French and circulated around

Europe. *Le Bibliophile Belge*, for example, appreciated Poe's combination of pathos and logic to create a masterfully original tale.[32]

After the success of 'The Gold Bug', Poe revived plans for *Phantasy-Pieces*. William H. Graham – George's brother – agreed to publish it but insisted on some changes. Though he accepted Poe's organization, he wanted to change the title and decided to issue the collection in individual parts instead of publishing the multivolume work simultaneously. Part-by-part publication let publishers maximize profits while minimizing risk. Consumers accepted more easily a forty-eight-page pamphlet selling for pennies than a multi-volume work selling for dollars. If an edition proved unsuccessful, the publisher could quietly let it die. Such was the case with *The Prose Romances of Edgar A. Poe*, as the collection was retitled. The first part, which contained the complete texts of 'The Murders in the Rue Morgue' and 'The Man that was Used Up', appeared in July 1843. There was no second part.

Regardless of his various projects, Poe had not lost his fascination for the tourist, which he continued to explore in 'Morning on the Wissahiccon'. Published in early November 1843, this sketch articulates ideas Poe had been subtly exploring since 'A Descent into the Maelström'. It was in 'Morning on the Wissahiccon' that he coined the phrase 'natural lions of the land'. Tourists, he critiques, 'content themselves with a hasty inspection of the natural *lions* of the land – the Hudson, Niagara, the Catskills, Harper's Ferry, the lakes of New York, the Ohio, the prairies, and the Mississippi'.[33]

America, he suggests, offers much attractive scenery beyond its major attractions: 'There are innumerable quiet, obscure, and scarcely explored nooks, within the limits of the United States, that, by the true artist, or cultivated lover of the grand and beautiful amid the works of God, will be preferred to each *and to all* of the chronicled and better accredited scenes to which I have referred.' The 'real Edens of the land', Poe continues, 'lie far away from the track of our own most deliberate tourists'.[34] Instead of always looking for the sublime, people should seek out the beautiful, which they may find in many places, some quite close to home. Poe essentially gives everyone regardless of wealth or leisure the chance to enjoy nature. There was no need to go to the expense of travelling to distant Niagara or the even more distant prairies for the aesthetic appreciation of nature.

In terms of intellectual improvement, the edifying lecture provided an important form of middle-class wintertime recreation. It also gave authors an avenue of income that was typically more lucrative than writing. From November through February, many authors criss-crossed the nation, speaking at local athenaeums, civic centres, lecture halls and schools. The edifying lecture supplied entertainment and instruction to those who frowned upon more popular forms of amusement. Some contemporary authors – Emerson most importantly – became celebrities on the lecture circuit. Others disliked lecturing, which could be wearisome and which took precious time from writing. Poe had so far avoided it, but 'The Gold Bug' prompted numerous lecture invitations. He decided to take the plunge. On Tuesday, 21 November 1843, he delivered a spirited lecture, 'American Poetry', to a standing-room-only crowd at the William Wirt Literary Institute. He repeated his lecture in Wilmington, Delaware the following Tuesday but did not lecture again until nearly a month later, when he travelled to Newark, Delaware on 23 December to deliver 'American Poetry' at Newark Academy. Poe lectured at Baltimore on 31 January 1844 and at Reading, Pennsylvania on 12 March.

Poe could have been more aggressive in seeking lecture invitations. Herman Melville averaged two lectures a week from late November through February in the first year he went on tour, travelling as far west as Cincinnati. Poe's reluctance to visit cities beyond those within about a hundred-mile radius of Philadelphia partly stems from a growing awareness of himself and his personal limitations. He also hated to leave his wife, whose tuberculosis was growing noticeably worse. Poe sometimes fooled himself into thinking her ailment was only bronchitis, but in the midst of her increasingly frequent coughing fits there could be little denying its nature.[35]

As March gave way to April, Poe realized Philadelphia had nothing more for him in terms of literary employment. He decided to move to New York. Leaving Maria Clemm behind to take care of loose ends, Edgar and Virginia left their Philadelphia home before sunrise on Saturday, 6 April 1844. They soon boarded the train to Amboy, New Jersey, where they transferred to the New York steamer. The letter Poe wrote Mrs Clemm bristles with specifics. Remarkably, Virginia hardly coughed at all during the trip. He tore his pants on a nail at some point, but the journey was otherwise uneventful. Leaving Virginia on the steamer in the ladies' cabin, he went to find a boarding house. It was raining so hard he had to outlay a hurtful sum from their meagre savings – sixty-two cents – for an umbrella. The image of Edgar Allan Poe traipsing around New York alone on this cold, gray, rainy afternoon sheltering his threadbare jacket and torn pants with a shiny new umbrella is nothing short of Chaplinesque.

He found a house in Greenwich Street, where room and board were surprisingly cheap. A half hour later he was escorting Virginia to their new home. The room was unremarkable, but the board elicited lengthy description. His account of their first meal there is that of a man who has been hungry a long time: wheat bread, rye bread, teacakes, strong tea, elegant ham, mountainous piles of sliced veal, and, for dessert, three dishes of cake. 'No fear of starving here', he told Mrs Clemm with obvious relief. The feast continued at breakfast: veal cutlets, ham and eggs, bread and butter, and plenty of strong, hot coffee.[36]

There was no time for dawdling after breakfast. With Virginia showing signs of improvement, Poe could leave her alone and venture out on his own. 'The city is thronged with strangers', he

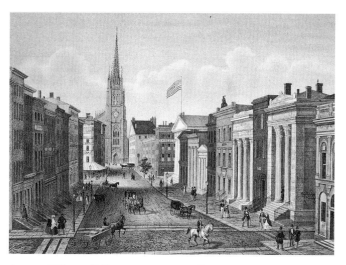

Augustus Köllner and Isidore Laurent Deroy, *Wall Street, NY*, 1847.

observed, 'and everything wears an aspect of intense life.'[37] For someone used to the peace and quiet of Philadelphia, the noise of New York was shocking. (It still is.) The din of the coal wagons and the cries of the clam and catfish vendors were especially grating. Poe had brought his newest story with him, the work later known as 'The Balloon Hoax'. He went to the office of *The Sun*, where he sold it to editor Moses Y. Beach. In realistic and highly technical terms, the story relates what was supposedly the first successful balloon crossing of the Atlantic Ocean. Beach published it as an *Extra* to the *Sun*. Resembling a genuine news story in terms of both discourse and typography, the hoax was a success, and many people accepted it as truth until they heard reports to the contrary. Unlike so many of his other stories of the early 1840s, 'The Balloon Hoax' does not comment on the tourist, but it does anticipate transatlantic flight.

A month after reaching New York, Poe had arranged with a smalltown Pennsylvania newspaper to contribute 'Doings of

Gotham', a regular column relating what was happening in New York. Before Thoreau ever said, 'I have travelled Concord extensively', Poe commented, 'I have been roaming far and wide over this island of Mannahatta.'[38] 'Doings of Gotham' culminates Poe's exploration of the tourist. Instead of scrutinizing the actual tourist as he had previously, he exemplifies the ideal tourist in 'Doings of Gotham'. Speaking as a Philadelphian on an extended visit to New York, he sees the city with the depth it deserves. Poe's ideal tourist closely resembles the *flâneur*. He proceeds slowly and deliberately through the city, observing closely and analysing what he sees: the birth of modern New York.

One day Poe procured a light skiff and rowed his way around Blackwell's Island on what he calls 'a voyage of discovery and exploration'. He wanted most to get a view of the picturesque Manhattan shore. Poe's vision was good, but his prescience was better. He shrewdly, if wistfully, saw the direction New York would take in the future: 'I could not look on the magnificent cliffs, and stately trees, which at every moment met my view, without a sigh for their inevitable doom – inevitable and swift. In twenty years, or thirty at farthest, we shall see here nothing more romantic than shipping, warehouses, and wharves.'[39] Ideal tourists do not let others determine what to see or how to interpret what they see. Like the *flâneur*, ideal tourists look carefully, but also think deeply. Refusing to accept the opinions of others, ideal tourists use their minds as well as their eyes to draw their own conclusions.

7

The Narrow House

'For the last seven or eight months I have been playing hermit in earnest – nor have I seen a living soul out of my family': so Poe told F. W. Thomas the second week of September 1844.[1] His words were not much of an exaggeration. After Maria Clemm had joined him and Virginia in New York, the three took lodgings with Patrick and Mary Brennan in their plain, old-fashioned, two-story farmhouse. Located atop a knoll on 84th Street, then part of the countryside, the Brennan home gave Virginia a place to recover her health and her husband a place to escape the pressures and temptations of city life.

Much as he had enjoyed the Wissahickon River and the surrounding countryside, Poe enjoyed the Hudson River and the woods that lined its banks. Mary Brennan remembered him as 'a shy, solitary, taciturn person, fond of rambling alone through the woods or of sitting on a favorite stump of a tree down near the banks of the Hudson River.'[2] Unemployed and impoverished since moving to New York, Poe saw little professional advantage in this self-imposed hermitage. In terms of literary productivity, however, he was well positioned during these seven or eight months to do what he did best: write short stories. With the success of 'The Gold Bug' the previous year, magazines welcomed his contributions. Relying on periodical articles to survive, Poe turned 1844 into one of his most productive years. By the time they moved to the Brennans, he had completed such new stories as 'The Oblong Box', 'The Premature Burial' and 'Mesmeric Revelation'.[3] He would write additional tales here and even return to his first love, poetry. The Brennan farmhouse no longer survives, but it remains famous as the place where 'The Raven' was written. But all Poe's hard work could not guarantee sufficient income, as the case of 'The Oblong Box' illustrates.

The previous year George P. Morris and Nathaniel P. Willis had revived the defunct *New-York Mirror* as the *New Mirror*. Eager to contribute to this periodical, Poe sent Willis a copy of 'The Oblong Box'. Knowing from past experience that periodical contributors generally were not compensated unless they stipulated so up front, Poe made it clear in his cover letter that he wished to be paid for the work. Willis greatly enjoyed the tale but said he could not pay for original contributions, suggesting Poe send it to *The Opal* instead. Poe was aware of *The Opal*, the annual giftbook John C. Riker published; the previous year he had published 'Morning on the Wissahiccon' there. But Poe generally disliked this annual. Since its contents were largely religious, reviewers of *The Opal* had ignored 'Morning on the Wissahiccon'. The sharp-edged

Samuel Hollyer, *The Brennan Farmhouse, 84th Street, New York*, 1909.

steel engravings that adorned the annuals offended Poe's aesthetic tastes. The engravings in *The Opal*, as one reviewer noted, were as 'stiff and cold as frozen carrots'.[4] The weeklies and monthlies also had a practical advantage over the annuals: they paid contributors more quickly. But Poe had idealistic reasons for preferring periodicals over annuals, as well. He wished to encourage the development of American magazine literature and foster the writing profession.

He called on Riker, who informed him that new editor Sarah J. Hale was now responsible for the contents of *The Opal*. Poe offered her 'The Oblong Box', asking if she would accept it sight unseen on Willis's recommendation. Realizing the unusual nature of his request, Poe supplied a reason for it: 'It cannot be improper to state, that I make the latter request *to save time*, because I am *as usual*, exceedingly in need of a little money.'[5] Poe's appeal to her sympathies worked. Hale accepted the story, informing him of her rate of payment: fifty cents per page – half what he had received from *The Gift* a decade earlier. Such meagre remuneration sometimes prompted authors to use underhanded means to maximize their earnings. Instead of sending Hale 'The Oblong Box' – the tale Willis had recommended – he sent her 'A Chapter of Suggestions', which consists of a series of random ideas on life and literature. He sent 'The Oblong Box' to Louis Godey. Since Hale was co-editor of *Godey's Lady's Book*, she recognized Poe's subterfuge, but happily it did not damage their working relationship. The list of suggestions appeared in *The Opal*, the tale in *Godey's*.

'The Oblong Box' takes for its theme the same general subject of many tales Poe wrote this year, namely the influence the dead exert upon the living. A fascination with death runs through Poe's work, but it seems especially acute in what he wrote in 1844: an indication of his fear over Virginia's worsening health. After booking passage from Charleston, South Carolina to New York aboard the *Independence*, the story's narrator is pleased to learn that his old college chum Cornelius Wyatt and his bride will be sailing with him. The narrator had not seen his friend since before the wedding and looked forward to spending time with them. Wyatt boards the *Independence* with a veiled woman, presumably Mrs Wyatt, and a mysterious oblong box.

Unaware of its contents, the narrator imagines that the box contains a valuable copy of Leonardo Da Vinci's *Last Supper*. Once the *Independence* wrecks at sea, all the passengers make it into lifeboats safely. When the captain refuses to save the box, Wyatt leaves the safety of the lifeboat and returns to the *Independence*. He lashes himself to the box, determined either to save or go down with it. The box drops quickly, taking Wyatt along with it. Afterwards, the captain explains that the box contained the body of Mrs Wyatt, who had died shortly before the voyage. The veiled woman was a stand-in. The switch was essential because, the captain said, 'Nine-tenths of the passengers would have abandoned the ship rather than take passage with a dead body.'[6]

'The Oblong Box' would seem to confirm the superstition that a dead body aboard ship brings bad luck, but Wyatt is the only person who dies in the aftermath of the shipwreck. And he dies not because of traditional superstition but because of a nexus of different factors involving the preservation of the dead. With advances in funeral science, it had become possible to preserve a corpse in a near life-like state for weeks.[7] Tuberculosis, strange to say, left many young, good-looking corpses in its wake. In addition, a craze for all things Egyptian, including and especially mummies, raged in Poe's America. Wyatt's foolhardy devotion to his wife's dead body leads to his own death.

Making Leonardo Da Vinci's *Last Supper* a motif in 'The Oblong Box', Poe broadened the theme of the dead's influence on the living. Christ's behaviour during his last supper established the pattern for Holy Communion, the rite that Poe had committed to memory as a youth in England.[8] 'Do this in remembrance of me': uttering this command while administering the sacraments, Christ gave all followers a ritualistic way to remember him. The painting itself represents another way the dead can exert an influence on the living: art. Poe's use of Da Vinci's fresco differs considerably from the way contemporaries treated it. In her poem on the painting, Lydia Huntley Sigourney, for example, conveys her reverence for Christ, then starts praising the painter, but stops short: 'I dare not muse / *Now* of a mortal's praise.'[9] Poe had no such qualms. He saw the artist – not just Da Vinci but any artist – as a god-like figure. Through the act of creation, an artist could transcend mortality.

The coffin forms a prominent motif in another story Poe wrote around the same time as 'The Oblong Box': 'The Premature Burial'. This story's general theme Poe found fascinating: he had used it earlier in such tales as 'Berenice' and 'The Fall of the House of Usher'. Poe was not alone. Many readers shared his fascination, as did the editor of the *Toledo Blade*, who reprinted 'The Premature Burial' in 1845. A month after reprinting Poe's tale, the *Blade* published a story titled 'Burying Alive'.[10]

The narrator of 'The Premature Burial' first provides a series of case histories of people who had been buried alive and then generalizes: '*No* event is so terribly well adapted to inspire the supremeness of bodily and of mental distress, as is burial before death. The unendurable oppression of the lungs – the stifling fumes of the damp earth – the clinging to the death garments – the rigid embrace of the narrow house.' Poe's words express his debt to James Macpherson's Ossianic verse, which had popularized the phrase the 'narrow house', a circumlocution for the grave. All the physical sensations associated with interment, the narrator continues, create 'a degree of appalling and intolerable horror from which the most daring imagination must recoil'.[11]

Suffering from catalepsy, the narrator builds several safety precautions into the family vault to guard against premature burial, but apparently he falls into a cataleptic state while away from home and is buried in a distant grave. Upon waking, he shrieks for help.

As it turns out, he has not been buried alive. Instead he has awoken suddenly from a sound sleep, not in the narrow house but in the narrow berth of a small sloop.

The experience proves therapeutic. He explains: 'I thought upon other subjects than Death. I discarded my medical books. "Buchan" I burned. I read no "Night Thoughts" – no fustian about church-yards – no bugaboo tales – *such as this*.'[12] The narrator's willingness to put William Buchan's *Domestic Medicine* and Edward Young's *Night Thoughts* behind him is understandable. Since its initial appearance over a half century earlier, Buchan, the most trusted medical handbook in America, had not gone out of print. Thousands of readers consulted Buchan for the purpose of self-diagnosis. Young's book, a classic of eighteenth-century British verse, exemplifies the graveyard school of poetry. Setting aside these two books, the narrator cures himself of both his hypochondria and his obsession with death.

'The Oblong Box' and 'The Premature Burial' can be seen as a diptych. Wyatt drowns because he refuses to let go of his dead wife's body. He symbolizes anyone who is brought down by whatever they cling to, be it an outmoded philosophy, excess cultural baggage, prejudice or an outdated aesthetic. Setting aside Buchan and Young, the narrator of 'The Premature Burial' puts the eighteenth century behind him, jettisoning his excess cultural baggage and saving himself. He explains, 'In short, I became a new man, and lived a man's life. From that memorable night, I dismissed forever my charnel apprehensions, and with them vanished the cataleptic disorder, of which, perhaps, they had been less the consequence than the cause.'[13]

A new man: this phrase recurs frequently in American literature. The ability to shrug off an old identity and take on a new one is a crucial aspect of the American national character. Perhaps the most startling line in the conclusion to 'The Premature Burial' is the one in which the narrator vows to read 'no bugaboo tales –

such as this'. As a writer, Poe himself was always maturing, always progressing, always taking new approaches. As 'The Premature Burial' nears its conclusion, it almost seems as if Poe has outgrown the story even before he has finished writing it. He wants to put it behind him and move forward.

Other stories Poe wrote in 1844 explore other ways the dead influence the living. Though Benjamin Franklin had debunked the theories of Viennese physician Franz Anton Mesmer more than a half century earlier, mesmerism underwent a revival in Poe's day. According to Mesmer, animal magnetism permeated the universe, attuning itself to the human nervous system. Nervous illness thus resulted from an imbalance between a person's animal magnetism and the external world. Practising mesmerists channelled animal magnetism through themselves to their patients. Some people believed that animal magnetism could put the living in contact with the dead. Given such bizarre ideas, Poe's imagination could work wonders.

In 'A Tale of the Ragged Mountains', the narrator tells the story of Dr Templeton – a practising mesmerist – and a patient named Augustus Bedloe. Between them, 'there had grown up, little by little, a very distinct and strongly marked *rapport*, or magnetic relation'.[14] Further distancing him from reality, Bedloe is also a morphine addict. While hiking through the Virginia countryside, he suddenly enters a city straight from *The Arabian Nights*. Simultaneously, Templeton is at home writing about one Mr Oldeb, a participant in the Benares Insurrection. Bedloe soon perishes from a remarkably similar wound to the one that took the life of Oldeb. Templeton, having channelled Oldeb to Bedloe, has apparently prompted Bedloe to repeat Oldeb's tragic death.

When Poe published 'A Tale of the Ragged Mountains' in the April 1844 issue of *Godey's*, he knew he had not exhausted mesmerism's imaginative possibilities. He returned to the subject a few months later in 'Mesmeric Revelation'. This story's narrator, another practising mesmerist, attends the bedside of a terminally ill patient, Mr Vankirk, one evening. He mesmerizes Vankirk and, in the belief that mesmerism places a patient in a heightened state of consciousness, quizzes him on several topics regarding the nature of God, heaven and the universe. A dialogue between the two occupies much of the story. Ultimately the narrator attempts to awake Vankirk from his hypnotic state only to realize he has perished under hypnosis. The narrator ends the story with a chilling question: 'Had the sleep-waker, indeed, during the latter portion of his discourse, been addressing me from out the region of the shadows?'[15]

'Mesmeric Revelation' intrigued contemporary readers. After its initial appearance in the August 1844 issue of the *Columbian Magazine*, one reader admitted being 'staggered' by the work and predicted it would be 'universally circulated'.[16] The prediction came true. The story reappeared in numerous American and British periodicals. The *Penny Satirist*, a London weekly, reprinted it as 'The Last Conversation of a Somnabule', introducing it as 'an interesting piece of composition, independent of all consideration of its truth or untruth'. Other periodicals seem inclined to take it as truth, including *The Dissector*, a New York medical journal, and *Evangelical Magazine and Gospel Advocate*, a biweekly religious journal out of Utica, New York.[17] From the curious to the devout, contemporary readers found something to like in 'Mesmeric Revelation'.

Poe was surprised by the reprints in medical journals: he had not intended the work as a hoax. He was pleased with the reprints in religious journals: he *had* intended it as an outline of his theories about God and the universe. Prior to the story's appearance, he paraphrased its cosmology for Dr Thomas Holley Chivers: 'There is no such thing as spirituality. God is material. All things are material; yet the matter of God has all the qualities which we attribute to spirit: thus the difference is scarcely more than of words. There is a matter without particles – of no atomic composition: this is God. It permeates and impels all things, and thus *is* all things in itself.'[18] To be sure, Poe never read that in his *Book of Common Prayer*.

Chivers, a physician and poet from Oaky Grove, Georgia, had been an ardent admirer of Poe ever since his *Southern Literary Messenger* days. When Poe announced the *Penn Magazine* in 1840, Chivers took the opportunity to initiate a correspondence. Seeing him as a potential backer, Poe cultivated his friendship. Chivers refrained from giving Poe the necessary financial support for his planned magazine, but his enthusiasm for Poe's art and ideas never withered. The letter about 'Mesmeric Revelation' gave Chivers great 'intellectual delight – the highest pleasure that a man can enjoy on earth'.[19] Making this remark in a letter to Poe the fourth week of September 1844, Chivers eagerly anticipated reading 'Mesmeric Revelation' in the *Columbian Magazine*.

Patterned on *Graham's*, the *Columbian* had only been established in January 1844 but was so far going strong. The same could not be said for the *New Mirror*, which ceased publication that September. Try as they might, Morris and Willis could not keep their weekly afloat. Postage was their single biggest expense. Current rates for magazines were all out of proportion with newspaper rates. Consequently, they decided to publish a daily paper, turning their weekly into a newspaper supplement. The *Evening Mirror*, as the paper would be called, commenced publication on 7 October 1844.

An evening paper required much more editorial work than a weekly magazine. Willis needed help and, at Maria Clemm's instigation, hired Poe as his assistant. Suddenly, Poe's months-long hermitage ended. Years later Willis reminded Morris:

It was rather a step downward, after being the chief editor of several monthlies, as Poe had been, to come into the office of a daily journal as a mechanical paragraphist. It was his business to sit at a desk, in a corner of the editorial room, ready to be called upon for any of the miscellaneous work of the moment – announcing news, condensing statements, answering correspondents, noticing amusements – everything but the writing of a 'leader', or constructing any article upon which his peculiar idiosyncrasy of mind could be impressed. Yet you remember how absolutely and how good-humoredly ready he was for any suggestion, how punctually and industriously reliable, in the following out of the wish once expressed, how cheerful and present-minded in his work when he might excusably have been so listless and abstracted. We loved the man for the entireness of fidelity with which he served us – himself, or any vanity of his own, so utterly put aside.[20]

Willis was right. Working as an editorial assistant was a big come-down. But Poe's role as 'mechanical paragraphist' did not sap his creative energy the way more responsible editorial positions did. When Poe assumed the responsibilities of editor for the *Southern Literary Messenger*, for example, he stopped writing short stories. As Willis's assistant, he continued his creative writing on the side. The following month, in fact, he wrote 'The Literary Life of Thingum Bob', a hilarious send-up of periodical publishing. Amazingly, this tale anticipates William Burroughs' cut-up technique, which involved slicing up a manuscript, randomly rearranging the resulting fragments, and then publishing the work in all its rearranged randomness. In Poe's story, Bob explains his process of reviewing books:

These works I cut up thoroughly with a curry-comb, and then, throwing the shreds into a sieve, sifted out carefully all that might be thought decent, (a mere trifle); reserving the hard phrases, which I threw into a large tin pepper-castor with longitudinal holes, so that an entire sentence could get through without material injury. The mixture was then ready for use.

When called upon to play Thomas Hawk, I anointed a sheet of foolscap with the white of a gander's egg; then, shredding the thing to be reviewed as I had previously shredded the books, – only with more care, so as to get every word separate – I threw the latter shreds in with the former, screwed on the lid of the castor, gave it a shake, and so dusted out the mixture upon the egg'd foolscap; where it stuck. The effect was beautiful to behold.[21]

Written while Poe was Willis's assistant, this story shows Poe retained his sense of humour during the experience. So does 'Some Words with a Mummy', another prime example of Poe's literary humour. Describing the revival of a five-thousand-year-old mummy, Poe continued exploring his fascination with death while satirising contemporary life. Having resusicated Count Allamistakeo – for such is the mummy's name – the story's scientists question him about what his life was like, learning to their surprise that ancient Egypt possessed the basic attributes of advanced civilization. The scientists boast about many aspects of modern life, but almost every time, Count Allamistakeo tops them. When they brag about the 'marvels of animal magnetism', for example, the Count assures them 'that the manoeuvres of Mesmer were really very contemptible tricks when put in collation with the positive miracles of the Theban *savans*, who created lice and a great many other similar things'.[22] The 1840s was a time of great optimism in America, a time when many, if not most believed in progress. Despite its slapstick humour, 'Some Words with a Mummy' provocatively challenges the whole notion of progress.

During his time with the *Evening Mirror*, Poe also returned to poetry. In so doing, he created one of the most memorable poems in American literature: 'The Raven'. Imagining how a woman's death affects her lover, Poe continued in verse a theme he had treated in his recent fiction. As he says in 'The Philosophy of Composition',

US Lithography Company, *Mr Henry Ludlowe in The Raven: The Love Story of Edgar Allan Poe by George Hazelton*, 1908.

Evert A. Duyckinck, *c.* 1875.

the tongue-in-cheek story of how he wrote 'The Raven', the death of a beautiful woman is 'the most poetical topic in the world', and 'the lips best suited for such topic are those of a bereaved lover'.[23] 'The Raven' appeared almost simultaneously in both the 29 January issue of the *Evening Mirror* and the February issue of *American Review*, which was released the last week of January. It met with instant acclaim, being reprinted by numerous periodicals, memorized by countless readers, and parodied by wits, wags, and sundry poetasters.

The appearance of 'The Raven' in the *American Review*, a magazine published by Wiley and Putnam, closely coincided with the firm's decision to launch an exciting new series, the Library of American Books. Evert Duyckinck, who conceived the series, struck a deal with Wiley and Putnam this February. He would serve the firm as literary advisor, choosing titles, soliciting contributors, and promoting the series.[24] Duyckinck's keen literary sensibilities let him recognize some of the finest authors in the nation; the series would ultimately include works by Margaret Fuller, Nathaniel Hawthorne, Herman Melville, William Gilmore Simms and Edgar Allan Poe.

Given the notoriety 'The Raven' established for its author, Duyckinck approached Poe, asking him to contribute a volume to the series. Duyckinck's idea for a one-volume collection of tales was not exactly what Poe had in mind. Poe still hoped to see a collected edition of all his tales, which would now fill five volumes, he estimated. Ultimately, two Poe titles appeared in the series, a collection of short fiction and a collection of verse. By the end of March, *Tales* was in press. Duyckinck himself chose twelve stories to include. Poe disagreed with his selections but carefully revised the contents to make them mesh as a whole. If twelve literary works are gathered into a collection, Poe believed, the thirteenth work is the collection itself. Though Poe grumbled about Duyckinck's selection, he had little room to complain. Reviewers warmly received the volume, and Poe even made a modest profit from it. Duyckinck's decision to emphasize the tales of ratiocination prompted French enthusiasts to notice Poe and start translating his tales. *The Raven and Other Poems*, Poe's next title in the series, solidified his reputation as the most original voice in American literature.

Poe and his family remained with the Brennans into February 1845, but the journey between the farm and the *Evening Mirror* office in lower Manhattan – about five miles – became increasingly irksome. Seldom able to afford the omnibus, Poe often walked both ways. The notoriety of 'The Raven' was making more demands on his time, both socially and professionally. He decided to move his family downtown to a house on Greenwich Street.

While working for the *Evening Mirror*, Poe started contributing to the weekly *Broadway Journal*. This February he signed a contract with its proprietor to co-edit the magazine. Willis was fond of Poe and sorry to see him leave the *Evening Mirror* but understood that the new position represented an advance in his professional career. During his time with the *Broadway Journal,* Poe went from co-editor to editor and co-owner to editor and sole proprietor, borrowing heavily to acquire the magazine. As a weekly, the *Broadway Journal* was not his ideal magazine, but it was the first over which he exercised full control. Predictably, editorial responsibilities sapped his energy and prevented him from writing many new stories.

Instead, he republished most of his older tales in the magazine. Poe had two reasons why he republished so much of his earlier fiction. Unable to pay contributors, he refused to compromise his standards by accepting amateurish contributions. Better to reprint his own carefully crafted tales than to publish the uneven tales of others. As a storyteller, Poe prided himself on his versatility but realized that such versatility was lost on contemporary readers because his stories had appeared in so many different magazines over the previous decade and a half. They had been published too diffusely to make an overall impression. The five-volume edition he projected could have given that impression. In its absence, the *Broadway Journal* was the next best thing. Separate issues comprising one or two volumes of the magazine could be bound together to attract investors and subscribers to the ideal magazine Poe envisioned. He always saw the *Broadway Journal* as an intermediary, a stepping stone to *The Stylus*.

Week after week, old Poe stories reappeared in the pages of the *Broadway Journal.* He went all the way back to the Philadelphia *Saturday Courier* tales for source material. Ever the perfectionist, he revised these stories for republication, sometimes significantly. It is heartbreaking to consider how much of his energy went into altering these already excellent tales and cobbling together this mediocre hodgepodge of a magazine when he was near the peak of his creative powers, when he could have been writing new short stories.

Thomas Holley Chivers came up from Oaky Grove this year to see his newest collection of poetry through the press. While in New

York, he took the opportunity to meet his idol in person, visiting the boarding-house at 195 East Broadway where Poe and his family had relocated on Moving Day. Already planning to write a life of Poe, Chivers recorded their meeting in great detail. Even allowing for some creative reshaping on Chivers's part, his transcript of their conversations forms an invaluable documentary record of Poe's personal behaviour and manner of speaking.

When Chivers arrived, he found Poe sick in bed. They talked at length, Poe remaining in bed the entire time. Maria Clemm later admitted to Chivers that Poe was not really sick. Rather, he remained in bed feigning illness to escape a commitment to write and recite a new poem before the Philomathean and Eucleian Societies at New York University.[25] Anxious to hear Poe's views about the Romantic poets, Chivers did not let Poe's bedridden condition hinder their discussion. Anxious to obtain a financial commitment from Chivers for *The Stylus*, Poe kept the conversation lively and ingratiating. Chivers steered the conversation toward poetry; Poe steered it back to publishing. Eventually Poe indulged Chivers, and the two discussed the verse of the British Romantics at length.[26]

'How do you like Shelley?' Poe asked.

'I consider him one of the greatest Poets that ever lived,' said Chivers, favourably comparing Shelley to Shakespeare.

'In passion he was supreme,' Poe responded, 'but it was an unfettered enthusiasm ungoverned by the amenities of Art.'

'But it was the clairvoyant fortuitousness of intuition,' Chivers replied in his characteristically flamboyant manner. 'Like St John on the Island of Patmos he beheld his celestial Visions of the coming of the New Jerusalem of Man with the couched eyes of one of God's Holiest Prophets.'

'His principal forte was powerful abandon of rhythmical conception,' Poe countered. 'But he lacked just that Tennysonian Art necessary to the creation of a perfect Poem. You are mistaken in supposing that passion is the primum mobile of the true Poet, for it is just the reverse. A pure Poem proper is one that is wholly destitute of a particle of passion.'

'Then you admire Tennyson?' Chivers asked incredulously.

'Yes, I consider him one of the greatest Poets that ever lived!'

'My God! Poe! how can you say that?' Chivers exclaimed. 'Why, his Poems are as effeminate as a phlegmatic fat baby. He is the most perfectly Greek statuesque, if you please – in his conceptions of any man that ever lived since the days of Pericles.'

Back and forth they debated the merits of Tennyson before switching to a different poet.

'What do you think of Keats?' Chivers asked.

'He was the greatest of any of the English Poets of the same age, if not at any age,' Poe answered. 'He was far in advance of the best of them, with the exception of Shelley, in the study of his themes. His principal fault is the grotesqueness of his abandon.' Chivers brought up the names of a few minor poets before bringing the conversation to a close.

Throughout the summer of 1845, the *Broadway Journal* often required Poe to work fifteen hours a day, yet all his hard work provided little income. He did manage to scrape together sufficient funds to move his family from the East Broadway boarding-house to 85 Amity Street (now West Third Street), a more fashionable address near Washington Square. An invitation from the Boston Lyceum offered some much needed income: fifty dollars for writing and reciting a new poem at its anniversary celebration on Thursday, 16 October. Poe accepted the invitation. His commitment to the Boston Lyceum resembled the one he had failed to fulfil at New York University. Once again, he found himself unable to write a new poem, but this time he had no intention of feigning illness. Confiding to Thomas Dunn English, Poe explained that he would 'cook up something'.[27]

Instead of writing a new poem, Poe decided to take one of his old poems and rename it. 'Al Aaraaf', the poem he chose to recite, would now be called 'The Messenger Star'. On such occasions, two speakers typically participated. The evening opened with an orator whose speech provided the meat and potatoes, so to speak, and closed with a poet, whose verse provided the dessert. A large crowd gathered at Boston's Odeon Theatre that Thursday evening. Caleb Cushing spoke first, delivering an oration on the subject of Great Britain that ran for two and a half hours. Poe was not obligated to do anything more beyond recite his poem, but he prefaced 'The Messenger Star' by articulating his literary aesthetic, which took around fifteen minutes. After this prosy preface, he began reading his poem.

'The Messenger Star' proved more than many Bostonians could fathom. Before Poe completed his recitation, many people left their seats for home. A few sensitive souls stayed for the complete performance. Joseph Buckingham, the editor who had neglected 'Epimanes' so many years before, greatly enjoyed 'The Messenger Star', calling it 'an elegant and classic production' containing 'the essence of *true* poetry, mingled with a gorgeous imagination, exquisite painting, every charm of metre, and a graceful delivery'.[28] Thomas Wentworth Higginson – later Emily Dickinson's editor but currently a student at Harvard – had been looking forward to Poe's performance. The Wiley and Putnam *Tales* turned out to be a great favourite among Harvard undergrads, and Higginson and his classmates were eager to see Poe in person. They were not disappointed. Poe started reciting 'The Messenger Star' slowly, but partway through

his voice seemed attenuated to the finest golden thread; the audience became hushed, and, as it were, breathless; there seemed no life in the hall but his; and every syllable was accentuated with such delicacy, and sustained with such sweetness as I never heard equaled by other lips . . . I remember nothing more, except that in walking back to Cambridge my comrades and I felt that we had been under the spell of some wizard.[29]

Those who endured 'The Messenger Star' were treated with a reading of 'The Raven' afterwards. Once the formal programme finished, Poe went out with Cushing and some others. Over a bottle of champagne, Poe let slip that he had tricked the Bostonians by reciting a poem he had written in his youth. Word of Poe's trick soon went round the Boston literary circles. Save for the editor of the *Boston Evening Transcript*, few seemed ruffled by it. The readers of the *Boston Evening Transcript*, who, as T. S. Eliot would say, swayed in the wind 'like a field of ripe corn', would have forgotten their editor's rant in a few days and let the matter pass. But Poe would not.

Returning to New York, he used the *Broadway Journal* to chastise the Bostonians for their ignorance and naivety. Telling the story of his visit to Boston, he depicted his choice of 'Al Aaraaf' as a deliberate hoax, an effort to expose the Bostonians' ignorance of poetry by showing how they appreciated this greenhorn poem as a polished work of a renowned poet. Poe's deprecation of the Bostonians – the Frogpondians he called them, after the pond on Boston Common – was too much for them to take. The Frog-pondians lashed back. Poe emerged from this controversy looking petty and vindictive.

'The Facts in the Case of M. Valdemar', one of the few tales Poe completed since joining the staff of the *Broadway Journal*, forms the final work in his mesmerist trilogy. He published it in the December issue of the *American Review* and republished it in the *Broadway Journal* the same month. It, too, captured the popular imagination and reappeared in countless newspapers and maga-zines across the USA and Great Britain. One London publisher issued it the following year as a separate pamphlet, *Mesmerism 'in articulo mortis': An Astounding and Horrifying Narrative, Shewing the Extraordinary Power of Mesmerism in Arresting the Progress of Death.*

Possibly the most gruesome tale Poe ever wrote, this story relates a case history of mesmerism. P—, the practising mesmerist who narrates the story, is contacted by his friend Valdemar, who is near death. Valdemar offers himself to P— as the subject of a mesmeric experiment. P— intends to hypnotize Valdemar shortly before death to see what happens once he dies. Perishing under hypnosis, Valdemar relates the moment he dies. From his hypnotic state, Valdemar identifies the precise moment of death. He maintains his mesmeric state for months, though his body shows obvious signs of decay. After seven months he manages to speak again, imploring P— to take him from his mesmeric state. P— motions for Valdemar to awake, and 'his whole frame at once – within the space of a single minute, or even less, shrunk – crumbled – absolutely *rotted* away beneath my hands. Upon the bed, before that whole company, there lay a nearly liquid mass of loathsome – of detestable putridity.'[30]

Read in relation to Poe's life, 'The Facts in the Case of M. Valdemar' presents an allegory of the *Broadway Journal*. The magazine died at some point in 1845, but Poe managed to keep it functioning into the following year – just barely. Poe published the final issue on 3 January 1846. In the story, Valdemar's last words are: 'I say to you that I am dead!' In the *Broadway Journal*, Poe's last words appear under the title 'Valedictory': 'Unexpected engagements demanding my whole attention, and the objects being fulfilled, so far as regards myself personally, for which *The Broadway Journal* was established, I now, as its editor, bid farewell – as cordially to foes as to friends.' Poe had kept the *Broadway Journal* alive long enough to republish nearly all his earlier tales. He had nothing more to fill its pages. His showcase was built. It was time to put down his tools and look toward *The Stylus*, which he still thought would be his greatest work.

8

The Most Noble of Professions

Many people who met Virginia Poe spoke well of her. Mayne Reid, for one, called her 'a lady angelically beautiful in person and not less beautiful in spirit'. William Gowans, who reacquainted himself with the Poes upon their return to New York, praised her 'matchless beauty', lovely eyes and 'surpassing sweetness'. Like Gowans, those who described her beauty almost inevitably mentioned Virginia's big, beautiful eyes. F. W. Thomas, who also appreciated her graceful manner, said she had 'the most expressive and intelligent eyes I ever beheld'.[1]

Even as they noted her attractive appearance and kindly demeanour, family friends also recognized her frightful illness. Reid used deliberately romantic language to soften his portrayal of her tuberculosis. He observed, 'I well knew that the rose-tint upon her cheek was too bright, too pure to be of Earth. It was consumption's color – that sadly beautiful light that beckons to an early tomb.' Dr Chivers spoke more bluntly: 'She was not a healthy woman, as I perceived after a little acquaintance with her – as, at irregular intervals – even while we were talking – she was attacked with a terrible paroxysm of coughing whose spasmodic convulsions seemed to me almost to rend asunder her very body.'[2]

Despite her ethereal beauty and her terminal illness, Virginia Poe could be a forceful woman, as a poem she wrote her husband for Valentine's Day, 14 February 1846, indicates. She wanted out of the city and let him know it in a way he could appreciate: a thirteen-line acrostic, the first letters of each line spelling out his name. The poem expresses her desire for a cottage in the country, where 'Love shall heal my weakened lungs', where they could escape 'the tattling of many tongues'.[3] Her words acknowledge both her deteriorating physical health and her husband's deteriorating social standing.

Since its publication in January 1845, 'The Raven' had turned Poe into something he had both desired and dreaded: a literary lion. 'Raven', to use the nickname society gave him, became the darling of New York's well-to-do literary women, including one in particular, Frances Sargent Osgood. Though married to portrait painter Samuel Stillman Osgood, Mrs Osgood befriended Poe, and the two carried on a public flirtation. She addressed love poems to him, and he wrote verse responses to her and published their exchanges in the *Broadway Journal*. Is the speaker of her love poems a persona? Or do they express her true feelings? Poe took them seriously. Speaking of Osgood, he said, 'Her character is daguerreotyped in her works – reading the one we know the other.'[4]

Osgood's social behaviour confirms her personal feelings. She was a fixture at the soirées hosted by Anne Lynch, whose home at 116 Waverley Place attracted everyone who was anyone on the New York literary scene. A petite woman with girlish features, Osgood often tilted her face upward, gazing at Poe with quiet awe. Virginia's attitude toward her has gone unrecorded. Osgood asserted that she and Virginia were friends and that she enjoyed the company of both Mr and Mrs Poe when visiting their Amity Street home. But Virginia seldom attended the literary soirées, where Poe and Osgood seemed inseparable.[5]

Though the *Broadway Journal* ceased publication in the first week of January 1846, its demise did not affect Poe's standing as a literary lion. The recent release of *The Raven and Other Poems* reinforced his status as one of the nation's greatest poets. Since

Amity Street was only a short walk from Waverley Place, Lynch took advantage of Poe's proximity. In the second week of January, she asked him to help write invitations. Poe's signature lent cachet to an invitation, helping to persuade a hesitant guest to attend. Besides Frances Osgood and Edgar Allan Poe, the guest list for Lynch's 10 January soirée included Margaret Fuller, who had established her literary reputation the previous year with *Women in the Nineteenth Century*, and Elizabeth Ellet, a prolific poet and translator Poe had reviewed in the *Southern Literary Messenger* the previous decade. As New York society was fascinated with Poe, he was fascinated with it – but he was in for a shock. He had yet to understand the pettiness, jealousy and backbiting that can afflict the social elite.

He eventually decided to give the reading public an insider's view of New York literary society, an endeavour fraught with peril. He would present his exposé as 'The Literati of New York City', a series of incisive character sketches published serially in *Godey's Lady's Book*. One of Frances Osgood's most delightful anecdotes concerns the manuscript of 'The Literati', which she saw while visiting Amity Street one day.[6] Poe wrote the separate segments that comprise the work on narrow scrolls, each formed from individual strips of paper glued together end to end. He and Virginia unfurled the manuscript containing his sketch of Osgood, and it stretched all the way across the room.

Poe wrote much of his work on such scrolls. His habit of writing anticipates Jack Kerouac's use of scrolls by more than a century. Like Kerouac, Poe recognized a relationship between the physical process of writing and the literary product that resulted. As a creative medium, the written scroll lent continuity to a work that individual sheets could not replicate. Poe anticipated Kerouac in other ways besides his writing process. Best known as the leader of the Beat Movement, Kerouac coined the term 'Beat' as a double entendre, to mean both worldweary malaise and transcendent beatitude, two characteristics often attributed to Poe. Given his affinity to both Jack Kerouac and William Burroughs, Edgar Allan Poe could be called the original 'Beat' writer.

Like Kerouac after him, Poe never really fit into New York society. Neither did Virginia. The women who lionized Mr Poe snubbed Mrs Poe. Some pretended she did not exist. Elizabeth Ellet had a husband in South Carolina, but she, too, fell for Poe. She had no qualms about visiting Amity Street. With a notorious reputation as a snoop and a busybody, Ellet happened to read a suggestive letter from Frances Osgood to Poe on one visit. Afterwards, she persuaded Osgood to get the letter back. Anne Lynch and Margaret Fuller undertook the mission and headed for Amity Street to confront Poe. Offended by their meddlesome behaviour, he said Ellet should be more concerned about her own letters to him. Lynch and Fuller left with Osgood's letter, reporting to Ellet what Poe had said. She sent her brother to Amity Street. He requested that Poe either produce the letters or apologize for insinuating that his sister had written such suggestive letters. When Poe refused, Ellet's brother threatened him with violence.

Shaken by the threat, Poe went to see Thomas Dunn English to borrow a pistol. English refused, flippantly suggesting Poe had never received any such letters from Ellet. Offended by English's suggestion, Poe struck him. A full-blown fist fight erupted. Conflicting stories obscure the outcome. Though ten years older than English, Poe had proven boxing skills, but his increasingly frequent drinking bouts hindered his athletic abilities. Let's call it a draw. Even if Poe won the fight, he lost his social standing.

But Lynch and Ellet could not get rid of Poe, who continued to intrigue members of their circle. Though banished from Waverley Place, he remained an object of curiosity and a topic of conversation. When Lynch hosted a Valentine's Day party that year, one guest read a Valentine for Poe, and another read 'A Valentine', which Poe had written for Frances Osgood. It begins:

For her these lines are penned, whose luminous eyes,
Bright and expressive as the stars of Leda,
Shall find her own sweet name that, nestling, lies
Upon this page, enwrapped from every reader. (ll. 1–4)

This poem takes the form of a cross-acrostic. The first letter of the first line corresponds to the first letter of Frances Sargent Osgood's name, the second letter of the second line to the second letter of her name, and so on.

There is something unsettling in the fact that Virginia wrote a Valentine for her husband in 1846, but he wrote one for Osgood. In addition, Poe's cross-acrostic format is more sophisticated than his wife's simple acrostic. Worse yet, Poe expressed his admiration of Osgood's eyes: his wife's best feature! Understandably, Virginia Poe was sick of New York society, sick of what it was doing to her husband, sick of the tattling tongues that circulated rumours about Osgood and Poe, tired of the small-mindedness, tired of the stuck-up women who looked down on her. Elizabeth Oakes Smith, another local poet with a crush on Poe, said of his marriage, 'I have always regarded this marriage as an unfortunate one for the poet, who needs a more profound sympathy always, if he would sound the depths of his own genius.'[7]

To Poe's credit, he granted Virginia's wish. That spring he took her to Fordham and showed her the new home he had found. With the surrounding fruit trees in bloom, the cottage was beautiful. Smith snidely called it 'a little band-box of a house', but it was just what Virginia wanted.[8] 'The cottage had an air of taste and gentility that must have been lent to it by the presence of its inmates', said Mary Gove, one of the few members of New York society who stayed friends with Poe. 'So neat, so poor, so unfurnished, and yet so charming a dwelling I never saw. The floor of the kitchen was white as wheaten flour. A table, a chair, and a little stove that it contained, seemed to furnish it perfectly. The sitting-room floor was laid with

Benjamin F. Buck, *Poe Cottage, Fordham*, NY, 1910.

check matting; four chairs, a light stand, and a hanging bookshelf completed its furniture.'[9] Poe rented it annually for only a hundred dollars. On Moving Day, he and his family moved into the cottage.

Poe may have physically separated himself from the city, but 'The Literati' was about to create a swirl of controversy in New York's literary circles. Compared with his earlier writings, 'The Literati' is closest in spirit to 'A Chapter on Autography'. Whereas the earlier work discerns personality on the basis of handwriting, 'The Literati' discerns personality on the basis of other externals: attire, physiognomy and phrenology. Read in light of his recent work, 'The Literati' seems disingenuous. Revising his stories the previous year for the Wiley and Putnam *Tales*, Poe had systematically removed the references to phrenology. He cancelled the discussion of phrenology that had originally opened 'The Murders in the Rue Morgue', omitted a sentence about phrenology in 'The Black Cat' and deleted a reference to George Combe in 'The Man of the Crowd'. These revisions indicate the doubts he now had.

Regardless of his own attitude toward phrenology, Poe understood that many others accepted it, and he used their gullibility to his advantage. 'The Literati' incorporates much phrenological vocabulary to describe personal appearance. Poe claimed he was giving his 'unbiased opinion', but what he was really doing was using the ideas underlying phrenology and physiognomy to create an elaborate illusion, to make his biased opinions seem unbiased. Phrenology's pseudoscientific vocabulary gave Poe the freedom to say whatever he wanted to say. He could curry favour with some by admiring the bumps on their head and denigrate others by identifying flaws in their physique.

His portrayal of Evert Duyckinck in 'The Literati' provides a good example. By now, Duyckinck had become the most influential figure on the New York literary scene. A review by him could make or break an author's career. Staying in his good graces made good sense. Of Duyckinck's physical appearance Poe observed, 'The forehead, phrenologically, is a good one; eyes and hair light; the whole expression of the face that of serenity and benevolence, contributing to give an idea of youthfulness.'[10]

Poe took his revenge against Thomas Dunn English in the third instalment of 'The Literati', which appeared in the July *Godey's*, copies of which reached New York the third week of June. Critiquing *The Aristidean*, the magazine English briefly edited, Poe observed that 'No spectacle can be more pitiable than that of a man without the commonest school education busying himself in attempts to instruct mankind on topics of polite literature.' Whereas Poe had complimented Duyckinck's youthful appearance, he made English seem both older and more inexperienced than he was. As Poe well knew, English was only twenty-seven, but he said, 'Mr E. is yet young – certainly not more than thirty-five – and might, with his talents, readily improve himself at points where he is most defective.' To enhance the aura of objectivity, Poe added one more boldfaced lie: 'I do not personally know Mr English.'[11]

English had no intention of letting such insults pass without comment. On Tuesday, 23 June 1846, the New York *Morning*

Telegraph published 'Mr English's Reply to Mr Poe'. In the past, English had been Poe's confidante. Now, he shamelessly violated their confidence, exposing Poe's secrets, depicting him as 'thoroughly unprincipled', an 'assassin in morals' and a 'quack in literature'.[12] Later that same day English took his reply to Hiram Fuller, who, with Augustus W. Clason, Jr, had taken over the *Evening Mirror* from Willis and Morris. Fuller published English's reply in the *Mirror* that evening.

Poe responded to English in kind. Louis Godey, who had encouraged Poe to write a response, had not realized Poe's capacity for personal vituperation. He decided against publishing Poe's answer and offered it to John Du Solle, who published 'Mr Poe's Reply to Mr. English and Others' in the 10 July issue of the Philadelphia *Spirit of the Times* – not to be confused with the similarly titled sporting paper. Poe also brought suit against Fuller and Clason for publishing English's reply. His libel trial was initially scheduled for September but later delayed until February.

While the case was pending, the *Evening Mirror* published English's *1844: or, The Power of the S. F.*, a serialized novel telling how a secret political organization named the Startled Falcons attempts to fix a presidential election. Set in New York, the story includes several characters based on real-life literary figures, including a journalist and poet named Marmaduke Hammerhead: a cruel caricature of Poe. Making the character a drunkard, English showed that Poe's drinking problem was common knowledge. English also denigrated Poe's physical appearance. The previous year he had celebrated Poe's massive forehead, but he gave Hammerhead a 'broad, low, receding, and deformed forehead', thus shrinking Poe's organ of ideality to almost nothing.[13]

Poe took this novel as a challenge. Having met English's earlier reply with a reply of his own, Poe now met this fictional work with one of his own. Though insignificant in itself, *1844* contributes to American literature as the inspiration for 'The Cask of Amontillado'.

Whereas English sought revenge in heavy-handed satire, Poe transmogrified their personal dispute to create a short story that transcends time, place and personality. 'The Cask of Amontillado' is one of the great revenge tales in world literature.

Appearing in the November 1846 issue of *Godey's*, 'The Cask of Amontillado' was the first short story Poe published this year. Under different circumstances, the Fordham cottage could have been an ideal place to write, but other factors hindered Poe's creativity. Virginia's hopes of curing her weakened lungs were of no avail. Each time her condition seemed to improve, it only got worse. This up-and-down path of hope and despair adversely affected her husband, who turned to the bottle for solace. Earlier, Poe's drinking sprees had been separated by months, even years of sobriety, but now he had lost all control. And Maria Clemm, whose daughter required her full attention, had lost the ability to control her son-in-law.

By November, Virginia was in dire straits. Appeals for charity to support the Poes appeared in the New York papers. Poe endured the humiliation for his wife's sake. These newspaper notices brought some of the more sympathetic and useful members of New York society to Fordham to help. Mary Gove and Mary Louise Shew came over from Manhattan, and Mary Starr came up from Jersey City. Despite their hard work and good intentions, Maria and the three Marys could do little. Their task was a melancholy one. Instead of nursing Virginia back to health, they simply sought to make her last days more comfortable. On 30 January 1847, Virginia Poe finally succumbed to tuberculosis.

New York literary society went on as before. Two weeks later, sure enough, Anne Lynch hosted another Valentine party during which guests read poems to each other. This gala evening was a huge success. Eighty or ninety guests attended, including nearly all the city's notable authors – except Poe. Though still in mourning, he did manage to write one Valentine this year. Written to Mary

Louise Shew, the poem expresses his gratitude to her for comforting his wife during her last days. Exacerbated by depression and drink, Poe's own illness persisted through much of this year. Shew continued visiting Fordham to nurse him. Poe won his libel suit in late February, but it proved a hollow victory. He wrote little in 1847. 'The Domain of Arnheim' was the only new tale he published. As a revision of 'The Landscape Garden', it can scarcely be considered new. He did write one masterful poem, which many consider superior to 'The Raven': 'Ulalume'.

Like so many of Poe's finest works, 'Ulalume' began as a challenge. The Reverend Cotesworth P. Bronson, a renowned teacher of elocution, dared Poe to write something suitable for recitation, something allowing students to demonstrate their range of vocal expression. While the mellifluous sounds of 'Ulalume' answered Bronson's challenge, the poem's setting may have answered a personal challenge Poe set for himself. In 'The Philosophy of Composition', Poe said he considered setting 'The Raven' outdoors but concluded, 'A close *circumscription of space* is absolutely necessary to the effect of insulated incident – it has the force of a frame to a picture.'[14] Setting 'Ulalume' outdoors, he achieved a circumscription of space through the use of an overarching canopy of tree branches. Taking place on Halloween and relating the story of a distraught man who inadvertently visits the tomb of his dead lover, 'Ulalume' is the single best Halloween poem in American literature.

Poe is the poet of Halloween. But Valentine's Day makes a more useful holiday for retelling the story of his last years. By 1848, Anne Lynch's annual Valentine's Day party had become the highlight of New York's social calendar. Though Poe's name no longer appeared on Lynch's invitation list, she had a new lion this year: Herman Melville. Raven had given way to Mr Omoo. Also this year Lynch solicited verses from Sarah Helen Whitman, a Rhode Island poet and widow. Though Whitman did not yet know Poe personally, she admired his work tremendously. Detached from New York's literary scene, she remained unaware of the negative attitudes society held toward Poe and assumed he would be attending the party. She wrote a Valentine for him. Lynch passed it over to someone else to read aloud.

On Valentine's Day two years earlier, Nathaniel P. Willis and George P. Morris had established their newest magazine, the *Home Journal*. They continued their close association with the holiday in the coming years. In 1847, the day before Valentine's Day, they published a letter suggesting that a subscription to the *Home Journal* would make an ideal Valentine's Day gift. After the holiday, they published many of the Valentines recited at Lynch's party. In 1848 Willis again encouraged Lynch to submit Valentines from her party for publication. The *Home Journal* published dozens of Valentines from the party in a single batch, but Whitman's was not among them. Lynch explained to her: 'The one to Poe I admired exceedingly and would like to have published with your consent with the others, but he is in such bad odour with most persons who visit me that if I were to receive him, I should lose the company of many whom I value more.'[15] Whitman persisted, and Willis published her Valentine to Poe separately.[16]

When Frances Osgood read Whitman's poem, she winced with jealousy. Expressing her feelings to Whitman, she started with a clever metaphor and ended with a quote from Tennyson: 'I see by the *Home Journal* that your beautiful invocation has reached the Raven in his eyrie and I suppose, ere this, he has swooped upon your little *dove cote* in Providence. May Providence protect you if he has! – for his croak [is] the most eloquent imaginable. He is in truth "A glorious devil, with large heart and brain".'[17] Osgood's conjecture was premature. Raven had yet to swoop down on Providence. He did find Sarah Helen Whitman's interest in him alluring. Since she went by her middle name, Poe clipped out 'To Helen' from a copy of *The Raven and Other Poems* and sent it to her anonymously.

Whitman gradually captured Poe's attention over the course of this year. For the nonce he kept busy with the longest and most intellectually challenging work he had yet attempted. Having initially sketched out his cosmological ideas in 'Mesmeric Revelation', Poe developed them further, presenting them in February as 'The Universe', a long lecture he delivered to a select audience at the New York Society Library. After some additional tinkering, he submitted his manuscript to George P. Putnam, who accepted it. *Eureka: A Prose Poem* appeared in July 1848 to generally excellent reviews. Poe impressed readers with his breadth of scientific knowledge and his imaginative understanding of how the universe worked.

Whitman and Poe corresponded over the course of the summer, and he made plans to visit Providence. He arrived on 21 September 1848 and stayed until 24 September. Their shared love of poetry gave them much to discuss. They also shared a birthday. She, too, was born on 19 January – though six years before him. The age difference did not seem to matter to Poe. He proposed marriage, but Whitman, understandably, hesitated to accept such a sudden proposal. He returned to New York with the situation unresolved. Receiving an indecisive letter from her in early November, he impulsively decided to return to Providence. He dashed off a letter to her, promising to arrive Saturday night, 4 November. The keen mind that had plumbed the mysteries of the universe earlier this year had stopped thinking rationally.

Poe travelled to Providence by way of Lowell, Massachusetts, the home of Annie Richmond, a bright, charming woman Poe had met when he lectured there earlier this year. Poe had developed strong feelings for her, and she greatly enjoyed his company. As the wife of Lowell industrialist Charles B. Richmond, she kept their relationship platonic and advised him to marry Whitman. He reached Providence that Saturday highly conflicted and deeply depressed. Instead of seeing Whitman, he spent the night in his hotel: 'a long, long, hideous night of despair', he called it.[18]

Delusional as well as depressed, Poe apparently imagined himself in the role of the romantic lover in 'The Visionary', with Annie Richmond as Bianca and her husband as the old, cold-hearted Mentoni. On Sunday morning he bought two ounces of laudanum. An opium solution, laudanum was typically dispensed in drops, not ounces. Two ounces was enough to kill two people. Poe took the train from Providence to Boston. He had a plan: he would take half the laudanum and then send for Annie Richmond. It is unclear whether she was supposed to save him, witness his death or take the rest of the laudanum herself. Before he reached the post office, the drug took hold. He later told the story to Annie Richmond, but he remained reticent about this part of it. The next two days of his life were filled with unknown horrors as the near-fatal overdose of opium worked its way through his system.

He returned to Providence Tuesday morning. Angry with him for not showing up on Saturday night, Whitman initially refused to see Poe but ultimately relented. Family and friends had warned her away from him, and she refused his proposal. He saw her again the next day, but she would not change her mind. Poe returned to his hotel Wednesday night and started drinking heavily. Still drunk the next morning, he showed up on Whitman's street, boisterously yelling toward the house. To avoid further embarrassment, her mother asked Poe in but spent two hours calming him down and sobering him up before she let him see her daughter. Poe's behaviour could have and perhaps should have led to their estrangement, but Whitman now understood that he needed a stabilizing influence in his life and decided that she could reform him. To the shock and dismay of her family, she accepted Poe's marriage proposal, and they began planning their wedding.

Poe returned to Providence the next month to lecture at the Franklin Lyceum. On Wednesday, 20 December, he presented 'The Poetic Principle'. In this, the fullest elaboration of his aesthetic principles, Poe stressed the idea of art for art's sake, denounced the longstanding notion that art should both delight and instruct, and emphasized that the only object of poetry should be the 'Rhythmical Creation of Beauty'.[19] The lecture was a brilliant success. Nearly two thousand people attended, with Sarah Helen Whitman seated front row centre. His impressive performance reaffirmed her confidence in him, and she agreed to accelerate their wedding plans.

After urging her toward the altar, Poe suddenly seemed to get cold feet, behaving in a way certain to alienate her. When she had some friends over on Friday evening, 22 December, he showed up drunk, not crazy drunk like before but drunk enough for others to notice. Disappointed, Whitman made him promise to quit. They planned to meet Saturday morning. Before heading to her house, however, Poe ducked into his hotel bar for quick eye-opener. He had long since forgotten Thomas W. White's admonition against drinking before breakfast. Partway through the day, she received a note from a friend who had seen him at the bar that morning. She could not mask her disappointment. Neither one explicitly ended the engagement, but both realized it was over. Poe said goodbye to her and left Providence by train that evening. He never saw her again.

Birthdays, especially ones with zeros on them, are always a time for taking stock. On 19 January 1849, his fortieth birthday, Poe could see his literary goals slipping away. His numerous attempts to establish *The Stylus* had failed. During his recent courtship, his writing career had come to a virtual standstill, and he had little motivation to get it moving. This seemingly bleak situation would soon change. In quick succession, he received two offers destined to shape the rest of his literary life. Edward H. N. Patterson, the junior editor of the *Oquawka Spectator,* a weekly Illinois newspaper owned and edited by his father, took control of the paper's print shop on his twenty-first birthday, 27 January 1849. A great admirer of Poe's work, Patterson offered to publish a national magazine with Poe as sole editor.

In Patterson, Poe found the person he had been looking for ever since he first imagined his ideal magazine, someone with the resources and the desire to support *The Stylus*. Their ideas did not precisely coincide. Patterson wanted to publish a more egalitarian three-dollar magazine – so-called after its annual subscription rate – whereas Poe had always foreseen *The Stylus* as a more upscale five-dollar magazine.[20] Patterson's geographical location presented another problem. How could anyone publish a national magazine from Oquawka, Illinois? Throughout his literary career, Poe had been a staunch supporter of the literature of the American South and West, but when faced with the reality of publishing *The Stylus* so far west, he hesitated. Despite his misgivings, Poe ultimately accepted the offer – provided Patterson agreed to a five-dollar magazine. Patterson did, and the two began planning their partnership.

The other major offer Poe received this year came from Boston. Frederick Gleason, the publisher of the weekly *Flag of Our Union*, wrote to Poe in January 1849, inviting him to become a regular contributor and offering to pay five dollars a page. As a contributor to Gleason's paper, Poe would have a steady, if modest source of income, which would help fill the gap until he and Patterson could get *The Stylus* going. Poe accepted Gleason's offer and got to work.

In 1849, of course, the newspapers were filled with stories of Americans seeking their fortune in the California goldfields. The idea of people rushing west to dig for gold disgusted Poe. Though he had long dreamt of great personal wealth, he refused to compromise his personal standards for it. He only wanted wealth if he could get it on his own terms, that is, as an author, editor, and publisher. In a letter to F. W. Thomas in February, Poe celebrated the benefits of the literary life regardless of the poverty it typically entailed:

Did it ever strike you that all which is really valuable to a man of letters – to a poet in especial – is absolutely unpurchaseable?

Love, fame, the dominion of intellect, the consciousness of power, the thrilling sense of beauty, the free air of Heaven, exercise of body and mind, with the physical and moral health which result – these and such as these are really all that a poet cares for: – then answer me this – why should he go to California?[21]

Poe channelled his disgust with the Forty-Niners into two works for *Flag of Our Union*: 'Von Kempelen and His Discovery', a short story about a successful alchemical process that transmutes lead into gold and thus makes lead more valuable, and 'Eldorado', a moody and evocative poem that transmutes the quest for gold into a symbolic quest for any and all elusive goals.

The juxtaposition of Patterson's offer and Gleason's illustrates a central problem in Poe's literary life. Gleason's offer motivated Poe to excel by writing more short stories. Besides 'Von Kempelen and His Discovery', Poe wrote three additional tales for *Flag of Our Union*: 'Landor's Cottage', which describes another idealized landscape in the manner of 'The Domain of Arnheim'; 'X-ing a Paragrab', a hilarious send-up of printers, publishers and the futility of literary quarrels; and 'Hop-Frog', another great revenge tale and, indeed, Poe's final masterpiece. In short, Gleason's offer prompted a burst of creativity, the likes of which Poe had not seen in years. In four months, Poe published more new stories than he had during the three years previous. And what resulted from Poe's association with Patterson? Nothing.

Though well intended, Patterson's offer was made without him knowing Poe personally. Like Sarah Helen Whitman, he formed his initial opinion of Poe based solely on his written work. But as Whitman could have told Patterson by now, Poe the man differed greatly from Poe the poet. Patterson wanted to meet Poe in person to finalize their plans for *The Stylus* and invited him to Oquawka. Had Patterson really known Poe, he never would have asked him to undertake such a lengthy solo journey, which involved untold dangers for anyone with Poe's personal weakness. Poe nevertheless agreed to visit Illinois.

After critiquing the Forty-Niners earlier this year, Poe, ironically enough, found himself heading west to find his fortune. He planned to lecture along the way to help finance the trip and solicit subscriptions for *The Stylus*. He would first travel from New York to Richmond. Then a combination land and river journey would take him to western Illinois. In earlier attempts to recruit magazine subscribers, Poe had found readers in the South and West particularly supportive. He was counting on their support again. The journey made good sense to Patterson, who sent Poe fifty dollars to help defray his expenses.

On Saturday, 30 June 1849, less than twenty-four hours after leaving New York, Poe was drunk in Philadelphia. After spending some hours in Moyamensing Prison for public drunkenness he was released. A cholera epidemic raged, and Philadelphia seemed deserted. He located some old friends, but they could do little to dispel the paranoid delusions haunting him. Convinced that some mysterious men were chasing him, Poe wanted to leave Philadelphia for Richmond, but two weeks passed before he could escape the city.

Poe routed his journey through Richmond partly because he had learned that childhood sweetheart Elmira Royster Shelton was now the Widow Shelton. He envisioned her as the new Mrs Poe. Upon reaching Richmond, he renewed their acquaintance. The story of their relationship does not take long to tell because it is almost identical to the story of Poe's relationship with Sarah Helen Whitman. After seeing her briefly, he proposes marriage. Startled by his suddenness, she hesitates to accept. He delivers 'The Poetic Principle' to a large audience. With other members of the audience, she is impressed by his performance. He gets drunk. She tentatively accepts his marriage proposal but insists he quit drinking. He promises to quit. This time, Poe took an extra step to help guarantee his promise. The last week of August he joined the Sons of Temperance and took the pledge to abstain from alcohol.

Settling down in Richmond, Poe kept his pledge and achieved a degree of equanimity he had not experienced for some time. The local chapter of the Sons of Temperance provided a powerful support network, and made it almost impossible for him to drink. The Widow Shelton noticed his improved behaviour, and their engagement became less tentative and more sure. In late September, Poe decided to return to New York, collect Mrs Clemm, and bring her to Richmond to stay. On Thursday, 27 September, he left Richmond on a steamer bound for Baltimore.

Poe's whereabouts between the time he boarded the steamer early Thursday morning and the time Joseph W. Walker, a local printer, sighted him the following Wednesday remains a mystery. One thing seems sure: after more than a month of sobriety, Poe reached Baltimore dying for a drink. Perhaps he headed for Widow Meagher's oyster bar. Or perhaps he stopped at the first tavern he saw. When Walker noticed him on Wednesday, 3 October in Gunner's Hall, a tavern on East Lombard Street, Poe looked like he had been on a bender for days. It was Election Day, and Gunner's Hall was being used as the polling place for Baltimore's Fourth Ward. Taverns made convenient polling places: campaign workers could treat to a glass of spirits whomever promised to vote for their candidate. Poe could be sure of finagling a free drink here.

Walker sent an urgent message to Poe's old friend Joseph Snodgrass, who came as quickly as he heard. Snodgrass recalled:

When I entered the bar-room of the house, I instantly recognized the face of one whom I had often seen and knew well, although it wore an aspect of vacant stupidity which made me shudder. The intellectual flash of his eye had vanished, or rather had been quenched in the bowl; but the broad, capacious forehead of the author of 'The Raven' . . . was still there, with a width, in the region of ideality, such as few men have ever possessed.[22]

Poe was so drunk he could hardly walk. Snodgrass and some others carried him to a buggy and brought him to Washington College Hospital. Dr John J. Moran, the attending physician, noted tremors of the limbs and constant talking: 'vacant converse with spectral and imaginary objects on the walls.'[23] Poe's condition worsened in the hospital. Deprived of alcohol after a long binge, he experienced acute alcohol withdrawal or the DTs, which can be fatal in extreme cases. Much mystery has surrounded Poe's final days, but the cause of his death is not hard to fathom. Hours before sunrise on Sunday, 7 October 1849, Edgar Allan Poe died of the DTs.

The tale of Poe's death is one of the most pitiful stories in the history of American literature. Instead of dwelling on it, let's return to a happier moment seven months earlier, when he wrote a letter to F. W. Thomas celebrating the literary life. Poe's letter responds to the news that Thomas was starting a new magazine, the *Chronicle of Western Literature*. Poe was thrilled to see Thomas turn editor: 'Right glad am I to find you once more in a true position – in the field of Letters. Depend upon it, after all, Thomas, Literature is the most noble of professions. In fact, it is about the only one fit for a man. For my own part, there is no seducing me from the path. I shall be *a littérateur*, at least, all my life.'[24] True to his word, Poe remained a littérateur until his death. His dedication to his craft, even in the face of debilitating personal poverty, is inspiring. The timing may be coincidental, but Poe wrote to Thomas on 14 February 1849: Valentine's Day. Perhaps this letter is the best Valentine Poe ever wrote, for it takes for its subject the greatest love of his life: literature.

References

Introduction

1 [John M. Daniel], 'Edgar Allan Poe', *Southern Literary Messenger*, XVI (1850), pp. 172–87.

2 Robert Louis Stevenson, 'Literature', *Academy*, VII (1875), p. 1.

3 W. T. Bandy, 'New Light on Baudelaire and Poe', *Yale French Studies*, X (1952), pp. 65–9.

4 F. Lyra, 'Poe in Poland', in *Poe Abroad: Influence, Reputation, Affinities*, ed. Louis Davis Vines (Iowa City, IA, 1999), p. 101.

5 Eloise M. Boyle, 'Poe in Russia', in *Poe Abroad*, p. 20; Rachel Polonsky, *English Literature and the Russian Aesthetic Renaissance* (Cambridge, 1998), pp. 97–114.

6 Sonja Bašić, 'Antun Gustav Matoš', in *Poe Abroad*, pp. 200–3.

7 Susan F. Levine and Stuart Levine, 'Rubén Darío', in *Poe Abroad*, pp. 215–220.

8 Kevin J. Hayes, 'One-Man Modernist', in *The Cambridge Companion to Edgar Allan Poe*, ed. Kevin J. Hayes (Cambridge, 2002), pp. 227–32.

9 Ibid., pp. 235–7.

10 Barbara L. Kelley, 'Ravel, (Joseph) Maurice', in *The New Grove Dictionary of Music and Musicians*, ed. Stanley Sadie and John Tyrrell, 2d edn, 29 vols (New York, 2001).

11 Kristin Thompson, 'The Formulation of the Classical Style, 1909–1928', in *The Classical Hollywood Cinema: Film Style and Mode of Production in 1960*, by David Bordwell, Janet Staiger and Kristin Thompson (New York, 1985), pp. 167–9.

12 Mary G. Berg, 'Julio Cortázar', in *Poe Abroad*, pp. 227–32.

1 The Contest

1 John Hill Hewitt, *Recollections of Poe*, ed. Richard Barksdale Harwell (Atlanta, GA, 1949), p. 19, which is the source of the following exchange.

2 Kevin J. Hayes, *Poe and the Printed Word* (Cambridge, 2000), p. 38.

3 'The Premiums', *The Bouquet*, I (1832), p. 31.

4 [Henry B. Hirst], 'Edgar Allan Poe', *Saturday Museum*, 4 March 1843, p. 1.

5 *Dover Gazette and Strafford Advertiser*, 28 June 1831; *Carolina Observer* (Fayetteville, NC), 13 July 1831.

6 Mayne Reid, 'A Dead Man Defended', *Onward* I (1869), p. 306.

7 Quoted by John Grier Varner, ed., *Edgar Allan Poe and the Philadelphia Saturday Courier* (Charlottesville, VA, 1933), p. 5.

8 'In the Last Number of the Philadelphia *Saturday Courier*', *Greenville Mountaineer*, 28 January 1832.

9 'Review of New Books', *Burton's Gentleman's Magazine*, V (1839), p. 169.

10 David R. Hirsch, 'Poe's "Metzengerstein" as a Tale of the Subconscious', *University of Mississippi Studies in English*, III (1982), p. 41.

11 'Literary Premium', *Cincinnati Mirror*, 29 September 1832, p. 7.

12 Theodore Besterman, 'Edgar Allan Poe's Occult Knowledge', *Theosophist*, XLVI (1925), p. 790.

13 Edgar Allan Poe, *Private Perry and Mister Poe: The West Point Poems, 1831*, ed. William F. Hecker (Baton Rouge, LA, 2005), p. 28.

14 Benjamin F. Fisher, 'Poe and the Gothic Tradition', in *The Cambridge Companion to Edgar Allan Poe*, ed. Kevin J. Hayes (Cambridge, 2002), p. 80.

15 Varner, ed., *Edgar Allan Poe and the Philadelphia Saturday Courier*, p. 10.

16 Victor Oscar Freeburg, *The Art of Photoplay Making* (New York, 1918), pp. 124, 156.

17 Sergei M. Eisenstein, *Selected Works*, ed. Richard Taylor, trans. William Powell, 4 vols (London, 1995), vol. IV, p. 463.

18 Varner, ed., *Edgar Allan Poe and the Philadelphia Saturday Courier*, pp. 23–4.

19 Kevin J. Hayes, *The Cambridge Introduction to Herman Melville* (Cambridge, 2007), pp. 116–17.

20 Varner, ed., *Edgar Allan Poe and the Philadelphia Saturday Courier*, p. 51.

21 Ibid., p. 59.

22 Augustus Van Cleef, 'Poe's Mary', *Harper's New Monthly Magazine*, LXXVIII (1889), pp. 634–40, the source of the following exchange.

23 Reid, 'A Dead Man Defended', p. 308.

24 J. Thomas Scharf, *The Chronicles of Baltimore* (Baltimore, MD, 1874), p. 93; John E. Semmes, *John H. B. Latrobe and His Times, 1803–1891* (Baltimore, MD, 1917), p. 105.

25 'Edgar Allan Poe', *Boston Daily Advertiser*, 24 September, 1878.

26 Lambert A. Wilmer, *Merlin: Baltimore, 1827*, ed. Thomas Ollive Mabbott (New York, 1941), p. 30.

27 Quoted by Alexander Hammond, 'Edgar Allan Poe's *Tales of the Folio Club*: The Evolution of a Lost Book', in *Poe at Work: Seven Textual Studies*, ed. Benjamin Franklin Fisher (Baltimore, MD, 1978), p. 18.

28 Frank Luther Mott, *A History of American Magazines*, 5 vols (Cambridge, MA, 1938–68), vol. I, pp. 599–600.

29 Poe to Joseph T. and Edwin Buckingham, 4 May 1833, in Edgar Allan Poe, *Letters*, ed. John Ward Ostrom, 2 vols (New York, 1966), vol. I, p. 54.

30 Semmes, *John H. B. Latrobe and His Times, 1803–1891*, p. 560.

31 Dwight Thomas and David K. Jackson, *The Poe Log: A Documentary Life of Edgar Allan Poe, 1809–1849* (Boston, MA, 1987), p. 132.

32 Semmes, *John H. B. Latrobe and His Times, 1803–1891*, p. 563.

33 Jorge Luis Borges, *Seven Conversations with Jorge Luis Borges*, ed. Fernando Sorrentino, trans. Clark M. Zlotchew (Troy, NY, 1982), p. 83.

2 The Birth of a Poet

1 Dwight Thomas and David K. Jackson, *The Poe Log: A Documentary Life of Edgar Allan Poe, 1809–1849* (Boston, MA, 1987), p. 11.

2 Ibid., p. 13.

3 Ibid., p. 26.

4 Kevin J. Hayes, *Poe and the Printed Word* (Cambridge, 2000), pp. 3–5.

5 Edgar Allan Poe, *Collected Works*, ed. Thomas Ollive Mabbott, 3 vols (Cambridge, MA, 1969–78), vol. I, pp. 427–8.

6 Hayes, *Poe and the Printed Word*, pp. 5–6.

7 Thomas and Jackson, *The Poe Log*, p. 47.

8 John T. L. Preston, 'Some Reminiscences of Edgar A. Poe as a Schoolboy' in *Edgar Allan Poe: A Memorial Volume*, ed. Sara Sigourney Rice (Baltimore, MD, 1877), p. 37.

9 Ibid., p. 39; Thomas and Jackson, *The Poe Log*, p. 47.

10 Preston, 'Some Reminiscences of Edgar A. Poe as a Schoolboy', p. 38.

11 Thomas and Jackson, *The Poe Log*, pp. 59–60.

12 Preston, 'Some Reminiscences of Edgar A. Poe as a Schoolboy', p. 41.

13 Thomas and Jackson, *The Poe Log*, p. 58.

14 Ibid., p. 65.

15 Quoted by Kevin J. Hayes, *The Road to Monticello: The Life and Mind of Thomas Jefferson* (Oxford, 2008), p. 626.

16 Thomas and Jackson, *The Poe Log*, p. 75.

17 Ibid., p. 70.

18 Hayes, *Road to Monticello*, p. 632.

19 Henry Tutwiler, 'Thomas Jefferson', *Southern Opinion*, 17 October 1868.

20 Theodore Pease Stearns, 'A Prohibitionist Shakes Dice with Poe', *Outlook*, 1 September 1920, p. 25.

21 Poe to John Allan, 21 September 1826, in Edgar Allan Poe, *Letters*, ed. John Ward Ostrom, 2 vols (New York, 1966), vol. I, p. 6.

22 Robley Dunglison, 'At a Public Examination', *Richmond Enquirer*, 27 December 1826.

23 Thomas and Jackson, *The Poe Log*, p. 74.

24 Stearns, 'A Prohibitionist Shakes Dice with Poe', p. 25.

25 Edgar Allan Poe, *Private Perry and Mister Poe: The West Point Poems, 1831*, ed. William F. Hecker (Baton Rouge, LA, 2005), p. xxix.

26 Ibid., p. xxxiv.

27 [Manuel Eduardo de Gorostiza], 'On the Modern Spanish Theatre', *New Monthly Magazine* VII (1824), p. 331.

28 'Notes for Bibliophiles', *Dial* LXII (1917), pp. 448.

29 Ulysses S. Grant, *Memoirs and Selected Letters* (New York, 1990), p. 31.

30 Thomas and Jackson, *The Poe Log*, p. 114.

31 [Henry B. Hirst], 'Edgar Allan Poe', *Saturday Museum*, 4 March 1843, p. 1.

32 Hayes, *Poe and the Printed Word*, pp. 26–7.

33 Stearns, 'A Prohibitionist Shakes Dice with Poe', p. 25.

34 Poe, *Private Perry*, p. 14.

35 Frederick Locker-Lampson, *The Rowfant Library: A Catalogue of the Printed Books, Manuscripts, Autograph Letters, Drawings and Pictures* (London, 1886), p. 189; 'To Helen', *Saturday Evening Post*, 21 May 1831; 'We Extract the Following Poetry', *Atkinson's Casket*, May 1831, pp. 239–40.

36 *Baltimore Gazette and Daily Advertiser*, 28 and 29 April 1831; 'Poems by Edgar A. Poe', *Baltimore Patriot*, 30 April 1831.

3 The Gothic Woman

1 Benjamin F. Fisher, 'Poe and the Gothic Tradition', in *The Cambridge Companion to Edgar Allan Poe*, ed. Kevin J. Hayes (Cambridge, 2002), pp. 82–3.

2 John Gribbel, *Autograph Letters, Manuscripts and Rare Books: The Entire Collection of the Late John Gribbel, Philadelphia* (New York, 1940), lot 544.

3 Poe to John P. Kennedy, 11 September 1835, in Edgar Allan Poe, *Letters*, ed. John Ward Ostrom, 2 vols (New York, 1966), vol. I, p. 74.

4 'The Baltimore Book', *Baltimore Monument* II (1837), p. 68.

5 'The Gift', *Cincinnati Mirror* IV (1835), p. 346.

6 Washington Irving, 'An Unwritten Drama of Lord Byron', in *The Gift: A Christmas and New Year's Present for 1836*, ed. Eliza Leslie (Philadelphia, PA, 1835), p. 171.

7 Poe to Washington Irving, 12 October 1839, in *Letters*, vol. II, p. 689.

8 Geoffrey Rans, *Edgar Allan Poe* (Edinburgh, 1965), p. 29.

9 Dwight Thomas and David K. Jackson, *The Poe Log: A Documentary Life of Edgar Allan Poe, 1809–1849* (Boston, MA, 1987), p. 149.

10 Poe to Thomas W. White, 30 April 1835, in *Letters*, vol. I, p. 57.

11 Ibid., pp. 57–8.

12 Edgar Allan Poe, *Collected Works*, ed. Thomas Ollive Mabbott, 3 vols (Cambridge, MA, 1969–1978), vol. II, p. 210.

13 Poe to John P. Kennedy, 11 February 1836, in *Letters*, vol. I, p. 84.

14 Lambert A. Wilmer, *Merlin: Baltimore, 1827*, ed. Thomas Ollive Mabbott (New York, 1941), p. 34.

15 Thomas W. White to Poe, 29 September 1835, in Edgar Allan Poe, *The Complete Works of Edgar Allan Poe*, ed. James A. Harrison, 17 vols (New York, 1902), vol. XVII, p. 21.

16 Wilmer, *Merlin*, p. 34.

17 Thomas and Jackson, *The Poe Log*, p. 171.

18 John P. Kennedy to Poe, 19 September 1835, in Poe, *Complete Works*, vol. XVII, p. 19.

19 Thomas W. White to Poe, 29 September 1835, in Poe, *Complete Works*, vol. XVII, p. 20.

20 Edgar Allan Poe, *Essays and Reviews*, ed. G. R. Thompson (New York, 1984), p. 778.

21 Salvador Dalí, *Maniac Eyeball: The Unspeakable Confessions of Salvador Dalí*, trans. André Parinaud (London, 2004); Dalí, *The Secret Life of Salvador Dali* [1942] (New York, 1993), p. 23.

22 Poe, *Essays*, p. 539.

23 Jean Cocteau, *Past Tense*, ed. Pierre Chanel, trans. Richard Howard, 2 vols (New York, 1987), vol. I, p. 37.

24 Thomas and Jackson, *The Poe Log*, p. 208.

25 Quoted by Arthur Hobson Quinn, *Edgar Allan Poe: A Critical Biography* (New York, 1941), p. 251.

26 Quoted by [Henry B. Hirst], 'Edgar Allan Poe', *Saturday Museum*, 4 March 1843, p. 1.

27 Poe, *Complete Works*, vol. XV, pp. 181–2.

28 Kevin J. Hayes, *Poe and the Printed Word* (Cambridge, 2000), p. 45–7.

29 Ibid., pp. 65–6.

30 Poe to James Kirke Paulding, 19 July 1838, in *Letters*, vol. II, p. 681.

31 Thomas and Jackson, *The Poe Log*, p. 248.

32 Poe to Evert A. Duyckinck, 8 January 1846, in *Letters*, vol. II, p. 309.

4 Making a Name

1 Poe to Nathan C. Brooks, 4 September 1838, in Edgar Allan Poe, *Letters*, ed. John Ward Ostrom, 2 vols (New York, 1966), vol. I, p. 111.

2 N. P. Willis, 'Letters from Under a Bridge', *New-York Mirror*, 1 December 1838, p. 180.

3 Poe to John Allan, 29 May 1829, in *Letters*, vol. I, p. 20.

4 Edgar Allan Poe, *Private Perry and Mister Poe: The West Point Poems, 1831*, ed. William F. Hecker (Baton Rouge, LA, 2005), p. 16.

5 Poe to James Fenimore Cooper, 7 June 1836, in *Letters*, vol. I, p. 94.

6 Poe to Nathan C. Brooks, 4 September 1838, in *Letters*, vol. I, p. 112.

7 'American Museum of Literature and the Fine Arts', [Charlestown] *Virginia Free Press*, 19 January 1839.

8 Edgar Allan Poe, *Collected Works*, ed. Thomas Ollive Mabbott, 3 vols (Cambridge, MA, 1969–78), vol. II, p. 334.

9 Ibid., pp. 338, 340.

10 Mary Louise Shew, *Water-Cure for Ladies*, ed. Joel Shew (New York, 1844), pp. 94–5.

11 Poe, *Collected Works*, vol. II, pp. 335–6.

12 Henry Watterson, quoted by Eugénie Paul Jefferson, *Intimate Recollections of Joseph Jefferson* (New York, 1909), p. 349.

13 Dwight Thomas and David K. Jackson, *The Poe Log: A Documentary Life of Edgar Allan Poe, 1809–1849* (Boston, MA, 1987), p. 254.

14 Ibid., p. 262.

15 Thomas Dunn English, 'Reminiscences of Poe', *Independent*, XLIII (1896), p. 1415.

16 Thomas and Jackson, *The Poe Log*, p. 265.

17 Ibid., p. 266.

18 Ibid., p. 268.

19 Poe, *Collected Works*, vol. II, pp. 386, 388.

20 Thomas and Jackson, *The Poe Log*, p. 274.

21 Poe to Joseph E. Snodgrass, 17 June 1840, in *Letters*, vol. I, pp. 137–8.

22 Geoffrey Rans, *Edgar Allan Poe* (Edinburgh, 1965), p. 1.

23 Thomas and Jackson, *The Poe Log*, p. 278.

24 Ibid., pp. 276–7.

25 Charles W. Frederickson, *Catalogue, Part First-[Second] of the Collection of Books, Autographs, &c., the Property of C. W. Frederickson* (New York, 1886–7), lot 1773.

26 Clarence S. Brigham, ed., *Edgar Allan Poe's Contributions to Alexander's Weekly Messenger* (Worcester, MA, 1943), p. 27.

27 Poe to Frederick W. Thomas, 23 November 1840, in *Letters*, vol. I, p. 148.

28 F. W. Thomas, quoted by Mary E. Phillips, *Edgar Allan Poe: The Man*, 2 vols (Chicago, IL, 1926), vol. II, p. 1010.

29 Poe to Frederick W. Thomas, 23 November 1840, in *Letters*, vol. I, p. 148.

30 Kevin J. Hayes, *Poe and the Printed Word* (Cambridge, 2000), pp. 70–73.

31 Poe to William Poe, 15 August 1840, in *Letters*, vol. I, p. 141.

5 From Peeping Tom to Detective

1 Dwight Thomas and David K. Jackson, *The Poe Log: A Documentary Life of Edgar Allan Poe, 1809–1849* (Boston, MA, 1987), p. 362; *Catalogue of the Books in the Library of the University of Sydney* (Sydney, 1885), p. 299; 'The Irish Gentleman and the Little Frenchman', *Bentley's Miscellany*, VIII (1840), pp. 45–8.

2 'The Irish Gentleman and the Little Frenchman', *Spirit of the Times*, 1 August 1840, pp. 254–5.

3 Kevin J. Hayes, 'The Flaneur in the Parlor: Poe's "Philosophy of Furniture"', *Prospects*, XXVII (2002), p. 103.

4 Clarence S. Brigham, ed., *Edgar Allan Poe's Contributions to Alexander's Weekly Messenger* (Worcester, MA, 1943), p. 15.

5 Edgar Allan Poe, *Collected Works*, ed. Thomas Ollive Mabbott, 3 vols (Cambridge, MA, 1969–978), vol. II, p. 500.

6 Brett Zimmerman, *Edgar Allan Poe: Rhetoric and Style* (Montreal, 2005), p. 76.

7 Edgar A. Poe, 'A Chapter on Autography', *Graham's Magazine*, XIX (1841), pp. 276, 282.

8 [George Combe,] 'On the Natural Supremacy of the Moral Sentiments', *Phrenological Journal and Miscellany*, III (1825–6), p. 337.

9 Edgar Allan Poe, *Essays and Reviews*, ed. G. R. Thompson (New York, 1984), p. 1208.

10 Poe to F. W. Thomas, 27 October 1841, in Edgar Allan Poe, *Letters*, ed. John Ward Ostrom, 2 vols (New York, 1966), vol. I, p. 185.

11 Nelson Sizer, *Forty Years in Phrenology: Embracing Recollections of History, Anecdote, and Experience* (New York, 1888), p. 181; Nelson Sizer, *How to Study Strangers by Temperament, Face and Head* (New York, 1895), p. 83.

12 [Thomas Dunn English,] 'Notes about Men of Note', *Aristidean*, I (1845), p. 153.

13 Kevin J. Hayes, 'Poe, the Daguerreotype, and the Autobiographical Act', *Biography*, XXV (2002), pp. 477–92.

14 Sammuel R. Wells, *New Physiognomy: or, Signs of Characters, as Manifested through Temperament and External Forms* (New York, 1871), p. 527.

15 Walter Benjamin, *The Arcades Project*, ed. Rolf Tiedemann, trans. Howard Eiland and Kevin McLaughlin (Cambridge, MA, 1999), p. 9.

16 Poe, *Collected Works*, vol. II, pp. 500–1.

17 Hayes, 'The Flaneur in the Parlor', pp. 104, 116.

18 Kevin J. Hayes, 'Visual Culture and the Word in "The Man of the Crowd"', *Nineteenth-Century Literature*, LVI (2002), pp. 445–65.

19 Poe, *Collected Works*, vol. II, p. 511.

20 Marie Bonaparte, *The Life and Works of Edgar Allan Poe: A Psycho-Analytic Interpretation*, trans. John Rodker (London, 1949).

21 Poe, *Collected Works*, vol. II, p. 515.

22 William G. Shade, 'Biddle, Nicholas', *American National Biography*, ed. John A. Garraty and Mark C. Carnes, 24 vols (New York, 1999), vol. II, p. 736.

23 Poe, *Essays*, p. 1146.

24 Poe to Charles W. Thomson, 28 June 1840, in *Letters*, vol. I, p. 140.

25 Poe to Nicholas Biddle, 6 January 1841, in *Letters*, vol. II, p. 694.

26 Thomas and Jackson, *The Poe Log*, pp. 318–19.

27 Ibid., p. 320.

28 Poe, *Essays*, p. 146.

29 Ibid., p. 148.

30 Poe, *Collected Works*, vol. II, p. 548.

31 Guy Debord, *Comments on the Society of the Spectacle*, trans. Malcolm Imrie (London, 1990), pp. 70–71.

32 Poe, *Collected Works*, vol. III, p. 979.

6 The Tourist's Gaze

1 James Buzard, *The Beaten Track: European Tourism, Literature, and the Ways to Culture, 1800–1918* (Oxford, 1993), p. 1.

2 Edgar Allan Poe, *Essays and Reviews*, ed. G. R. Thompson (New York, 1984), p. 1208.

3 'Trip to Niagara Falls', *Cincinnati Mirror*, 3 September 1836, p. 254.

4 Edgar Allan Poe, *Collected Works*, ed. Thomas Ollive Mabbott, 3 vols (Cambridge, MA, 1969–78), vol. III, p. 862.

5 Ibid., vol. II, p. 583.

6 Ibid., vol. II, p. 578.

7 Ibid.

8 John Urry, *The Tourist Gaze*, 2nd edn (London, 2002), pp. 3–4.

9 'Tourists in the Pyrenees', *Museum of Foreign Literature, Science, and Art*, XXIII (1838), p. 469.

10 Kevin J. Hayes, 'Baedeker Guides', in *Literature of Travel and Exploration: An Encyclopedia*, ed. Jennifer Speake, 3 vols (London, 2003), vol. I, p. 58.

11 Poe to Frederick W. Thomas, 25 May 1842, Edgar Allan Poe, *Letters*, ed. John Ward Ostrom, 2 vols (New York, 1966), vol. I, p. 197.

12 Edgar A. Poe, 'Eleonora: A Fable', *Great Western Magazine and Anglo-American Journal*, I (1842), pp. 43–6.

13 Dwight Thomas and David K. Jackson, *The Poe Log: A Documentary Life of Edgar Allan Poe, 1809–1849* (Boston, MA, 1987), p. 325.

14 Ibid., p. 370.

15 Ibid., pp. 355, 371.

16 Joel Benton, *In the Poe Circle: With Some Account of the Poe–Chivers Controversy, and Other Poe Memorabilia* (New York, 1899), pp. 58–9.

17 Henry Howard Paul, *Dashes of American Humour* (London, 1852), p. 136; Charles Fenno Hoffman, 'The Origin of Mint Juleps', in *The Poets and Poetry of America*, ed. Rufus Wilmot Griswold (Philadelphia, PA, 1856), p. 336.

18 Paul, *Dashes of American Humour*, p. 137.

19 Poe to J. and H. G. Langley, 19 July 1842, *Letters*, vol. II, p. 699.

20 Augustus Van Cleef, 'Poe's Mary', *Harper's New Monthly Magazine*, LXXVIII (1889), p. 639.

21 *American Book-Prices Current: A Record of Books, Manuscripts and Autographs Sold at Auction in New York, Boston, and Philadelphia, from September, 1919, to July, 1920* (New York, 1920), p. 661, lists a copy of Harding's *Principles and Practice of Art* with Poe's presentation inscription.

22 Poe, *Collected Works*, vol. III, p. 1281.

23 Miles Orvell, 'Virtual Culture and the Logic of American Technology', *Revue Française d'Études Américaines*, LXXVI (1998), p. 15.

24 Richard Burgin, ed., *Jorge Luis Borges: Conversations* (Jackson, MS, 1998), p. 196.

25 Edgar Allan Poe, *Essays and Reviews*, ed. G. R. Thompson (New York, 1984), p. 556.

26 Thomas and Jackson, *The Poe Log*, p. 380.

27 Quoted by Mary E. Phillips, *Edgar Allan Poe: The Man*, 2 vols

(Chicago, IL, 1926), vol. I, p. 749.

28 'Editors' Book Table', *Godey's Lady's Book*, XXV (1842), p. 250.

29 F. W. Thomas to Poe, 7 March 1841, in Poe, *Complete Works*, vol. XVII, p. 81.

30 Poe to F. W. Thomas and Jesse E. Dow, 16 March 1843, in *Letters*, vol. I, p. 229.

31 John Hill Hewitt, *Recollections of Poe*, ed. Richard Barksdale Harwell (Atlanta, GA, 1949), p. 19.

32 'Chronique et Variétés', *Le Bibliophile Belge*, III (1846), p. 144.

33 Poe, *Collected Works*, vol. III, p. 862.

34 Edgar A. Poe, 'Morning on the Wissahiccon', in *The Opal*, ed. N. P. Willis (New York, 1844), p. 250.

35 Thomas Holley Chivers, *Life of Poe*, ed. Richard Beale Davis (New York, 1952), p. 43.

36 Poe to Maria Clemm, 7 April 1844, *Letters*, vol. I, p. 252.

37 Edgar Allan Poe, *Doings of Gotham*, ed. Jacob E. Spannuth and Thomas Ollive Mabbott (Pottsville, PA, 1929), p. 31.

38 Ibid., p. 25.

39 Ibid., pp. 40–41.

7 The Narrow House

1 Poe to F. W. Thomas, 8 September 1844, in Edgar Allan Poe, *Letters*, ed. John Ward Ostrom, 2 vols (New York, 1966), vol. I, p. 708.

2 William F. Gill, *The Life of Edgar Allan Poe*, 3rd edn (London, 1878), p. 149.

3 Poe to James R. Lowell, 28 May 1844, *Letters*, vol. I, p. 253.

4 'Editors' Table', *Ladies' Companion*, December 1843, p. 104.

5 Poe to Sarah J. Hale, 29 May 1844, in *Letters*, vol. II, p. 705.

6 Edgar Allan Poe, *Collected Works*, ed. Thomas Ollive Mabbott, 3 vols (Cambridge, MA, 1969–78), vol. III, p. 933.

7 Judith E. Pike, 'Poe and the Revenge of the Exquisite Corpse', *Studies in American Fiction*, XXVI (1998), p. 172.

8 Kevin J. Hayes, *Poe and the Printed Word* (Cambridge, 2000), pp. 4–5.

9 Lydia Huntley Sigourney, 'The Last Supper', *Episcopal Recorder*, X (1833), p. 196.

10 Edgar A. Poe, 'The Premature Burial', *Toledo Blade*, 4 July 1845; 'Burying Alive', *Toledo Blade*, 15 August 1845.

11 Poe, *Collected Works*, vol. III, p. 961.

12 Ibid., vol. III, p. 969.

13 Ibid.

14 Ibid., vol. III, p. 941.

15 Ibid., vol. III, p. 1040.

16 'American Magazines', *New World*, 3 August 1844, p. 132.

17 Edgar A. Poe, 'The Last Conversation of a Somnabule', *Penny Satirist*, 8 November 1845, p. 4; 'Mesmeric Revelation', *Dissector*, I (1844), pp. 185–9; 'Mesmeric Revelation', *Evangelical Magazine and Gospel Advocate*, XVI (1845), pp. 364–5.

18 Poe to Thomas Holley Chivers, 10 July 1844, *Letters*, vol. I, p. 260.

19 Dwight Thomas and David K. Jackson, *The Poe Log: A Documentary Life of Edgar Allan Poe, 1809–1849* (Boston, MA, 1987), p. 470.

20 Ibid., p. 473.

21 Poe, *Collected Works*, vol. III, p. 1141.

22 Ibid., vol. III, p. 1191.

23 Edgar Allan Poe, *Essays and Reviews*, ed. G. R. Thompson (New York, 1984), p. 19.

24 Ezra Greenspan, 'Evert Duyckinck and the History of Wiley and Putnam's Library of American Books, 1845–1847', *American Literature*, LXIV (1992), p. 682.

25 Kenneth Silverman, *Edgar A. Poe: Mournful and Never-Ending Remembrance* (New York, 1991), p. 260.

26 Thomas Holley Chivers, *Life of Poe*, ed. Richard Beale Davis (New York, 1952), pp. 39–52, the source of the following exchange.

27 Silverman, *Edgar A. Poe*, p. 309.

28 Thomas and Jackson, *The Poe Log*, p. 579.

29 Ibid., p. 518.

30 Poe, *Collected Works*, vol. III, p. 1243.

8 The Most Noble of Professions

1 Mayne Reid, 'A Dead Man Defended', *Onward*, I (1869), p. 306; Dwight Thomas and David K. Jackson, *The Poe Log: A Documentary*

Life of Edgar Allan Poe, 1809–1849 (Boston, MA, 1987), pp. 242, 380.

2 Reid, 'A Dead Man Defended', p. 306; Thomas Holley Chivers, *Life of Poe*, ed. Richard Beale Davis (New York, 1952), p. 42.

3 Thomas and Jackson, *The Poe Log*, p. 625.

4 Edgar Allan Poe, *Essays and Reviews*, ed. G. R. Thompson (New York, 1984), p. 1197.

5 Kenneth Silverman, *Edgar A. Poe: Mournful and Never-Ending Remembrance* (New York, 1991), p. 284.

6 Thomas and Jackson, *The Poe Log*, p. 622.

7 Elizabeth Oakes Smith, 'Autobiographic Notes', *Beadle's Monthly*, III (1867), p. 155.

8 Ibid., p. 156.

9 Mary Gove Nichols, *Reminiscences of Edgar Allan Poe* (New York, 1974), pp. 8–9.

10 Poe, *Essays*, p. 1162.

11 Ibid., pp. 1166–7.

12 Thomas and Jackson, *The Poe Log*, p. 648.

13 Ibid., p. 663.

14 Poe, *Essays*, p. 21.

15 Thomas and Jackson, *The Poe Log*, p. 726.

16 Silverman, *Edgar A. Poe*, p. 349.

17 Thomas and Jackson, *The Poe Log*, pp. 729–30.

18 Poe to Annie L. Richmond, 16 November 1848, in Edgar Allan Poe, *Letters*, ed. John Ward Ostrom, 2 vols (New York, 1966), vol. II, p. 401.

19 Poe, *Essays*, pp. 71–94.

20 For a discussion of the differences between these types of magazines, see Kevin J. Hayes, *Poe and the Printed Word* (Cambridge, 2000), p. 93.

21 Poe to F. W. Thomas, 14 February 1849, *Letters*, vol. II, p. 427.

22 Thomas and Jackson, *The Poe Log*, p. 844.

23 Ibid., p. 845.

24 Poe to F. W. Thomas, 14 February 1849, *Letters*, vol. II, p. 427.

Select Bibliography

Useful Editions of Poe's Work

The Brevities: Pinakidia, Marginalia, Fifty Suggestions, and Other Works, ed. Burton Pollin (New York, 1985)

Collected Works of Edgar Allan Poe, ed. Thomas Ollive Mabbott, 3 vols (Cambridge, MA, 1969–78)

The Complete Works of Edgar Allan Poe, ed. James A. Harrison, 17 vols (New York, 1902)

Doings of Gotham, ed. Jacob E. Spannuth and Thomas O. Mabbott (Pottsville, PA, 1929)

Edgar Allan Poe and the Philadelphia Saturday Courier: Facsimile Reproductions of the First Texts of Poe's Earliest Tales and 'Raising the Wind', ed. John Grier Varner (Charlottesville, VA, 1933)

Edgar Allan Poe's Contributions to Alexander's Weekly Messenger, ed. Clarence S. Brigham (Worcester, MA, 1943)

Essays and Reviews, ed. G. R. Thompson (New York, 1984)

Eureka, ed. Stuart Levine and Susan F. Levine (Urbana, IL, 2004)

Letters, ed. John Ward Ostrom, revd edn, 2 vols (New York, 1966)

Poe: The Laurel Poetry Series, ed. Richard Wilbur (New York, 1959)

Poetry and Tales, ed. Patrick F. Quinn (New York, 1984)

Private Perry and Mister Poe: The West Point Poems, 1831, ed. William F. Hecker (Baton Rouge, LA, 2005)

The Short Fiction of Edgar Allan Poe, ed. Stuart Levine and Susan Levine (1976; repr., Urbana, IL, 1990)

Biographies and Biographical Studies

Allen, Hervey, *Israfel: The Life and Times of Edgar Allan Poe*, 2 vols (New York, 1927)

Chivers, Thomas Holley, *Life of Poe*, ed. Richard Beale Davis (New York, 1952)

Hutchisson, James M., *Poe* (Jackson, MS, 2005)

Miller, John Carl, ed., *Building Poe Biography* (Baton Rouge, LA, 1977)

—, ed., *Poe's Helen Remembers* (Charlottesville, VA, 1979)

Moss, Sidney P., *Poe's Literary Battles: The Critic in the Context of His Literary Milieu* (Durham, NC, 1963)

—, *Poe's Major Crisis: His Libel Suit and New York's Literary World* (Durham, NC, 1970)

Phillips, Mary E., *Edgar Allan Poe: The Man*, 2 vols (Chicago, IL, 1926)

Quinn, Arthur Hobson. *Edgar Allan Poe: A Critical Biography* (New York, 1941)

Silverman, Kenneth, *Edgar A. Poe: Mournful and Never-Ending Remembrance* (New York, 1991)

Thomas, Dwight, and David K. Jackson, *The Poe Log: A Documentary Life of Edgar Allan Poe, 1809–1849* (Boston, MA, 1987)

Walsh, John Evangelist, *Midnight Dreary: The Mysterious Death of Edgar Allan Poe* (New Brunswick, NJ, 1998)

Bibliographies and Indexes

Damerson, J. Lasley, and Irby B. Cauthen, Jr, *Edgar Allan Poe: A Bibliography of Criticism, 1827–1967* (Charlottesville, VA, 1974)

Deas, Michael, *The Portraits and Daguerreotypes of Edgar Allan Poe* (Charlottesville, VA, 1989)

Frank, Frederick S., and Antony Magistrale, *The Poe Encyclopedia* (Westport, CT, 1997)

Heartman, Charles F., and James R. Canny, *A Bibliography of First Printings of the Writings of Edgar Allan Poe: Together with a Record of First and Contemporary Later Printings of His Contributions to Annuals, Anthologies, Periodicals and Newspapers Issued During His Lifetime, Also Some Spurious Poeana and Fakes,* revd edn (Hattiesburg, MS, 1943)

Hyneman, Esther F., *Edgar Allan Poe: An Annotated Bibliography of Books and Articles in English, 1827–1973* (Boston, MA, 1974)

Pollin, Burton R., *Dictionary of Names and Titles in Poe's Collected Works* (New York, 1968)
—, *Images of Poe's Works: A Comprehensive Descriptive Catalogue of Illustrations* (Westport, CT, 1989)

Critical Studies

Brand, Dana, *The Spectator and the City in Nineteenth-century American Literature* (Cambridge, 1991)
Budd, Louis J., and Edwin H. Cady, eds., *On Poe* (Durham, NC, 1993)
Campbell, Killis, *The Mind of Poe, and Other Studies* (Cambridge, MA, 1933)
Davidson, Edward H., *Poe: A Critical Study* (Cambridge, MA, 1957)
Fagin, N. Bryllion, *The Histrionic Mr. Poe* (Baltimore, MD, 1949)
Fisher, Benjamin Franklin, *The Cambridge Introduction to Edgar Allan Poe* (Cambridge, 2008)
—, ed., *Poe and His Times: The Artist and His Milieu* (Baltimore, MD, 1990)
—, ed., *Poe and Our Times: Influences and Affinities* (Baltimore, MD, 1986)
—, ed., *Poe at Work: Seven Textual Studies* (Baltimore, MD, 1978)
Harvey, Ronald C., *The Critical History of Edgar Allan Poe's The Narrative of Arthur Gordon Pym: 'A Dialogue with Unreason'* (New York, 1998)
Hayes, Kevin, ed., *The Cambridge Companion to Edgar Allan Poe* (Cambridge, 2002, repr. Shanghai, 2004)
—, *Poe and the Printed Word* (Cambridge, 2000)
Hoffman, Daniel, *Poe Poe Poe Poe Poe Poe Poe* (Garden City, NY, 1972)
Kennedy, J. Gerald, ed., *A Historical Guide to Edgar Allan Poe* (Oxford, 2001)
—, *The Narrative of Arthur Gordon Pym: and the Abyss of Interpretation* (New York, 1995)
Kopley, Richard, ed., *Poe's Pym: Critical Explorations* (Durham, NC, 1992)
Ljungquist, Kent, *The Grand and the Fair: Poe's Landscape Aesthetics and Pictorial Techniques* (Potomac, MD, 1984)
McGill, Meredith L. *American Literature and the Culture of Reprinting, 1834–1853* (Philadelphia, PA, 2003)
May, Charles E., *Edgar Allan Poe: A Study of the Short Fiction* (Boston, MA, 1991)
Mills, Bruce, *Poe, Fuller, and the Mesmeric Arts: Transition States in the*

American Renaissance (Columbia, MO, 2006)

Parks, Edd Winfield, *Edgar Allan Poe as Literary Critic* (Athens, GA, 1964)

Peeples, Scott, *Edgar Allan Poe Revisited* (New York, 1998)

Quinn, Patrick F., *The French Face of Edgar Poe* (Carbondale, IL, 1957)

Rans, Geoffrey, *Edgar Allan Poe* (Edinburgh, 1965)

Richard, Eliza, *Gender and the Poetics of Reception in Poe's Circle* (Cambridge, 2004)

Rosenheim, Shawn, *The Cryptographic Imagination: Secret Writing from Edgar Poe to the Internet* (Baltimore, MD, 1997)

—, and Stephen Rachman, ed., *The American Face of Edgar Allan Poe* (Baltimore, MD, 1995)

Silverman, Kenneth, ed., *New Essays on Poe's Major Tales* (Cambridge, 1993)

Stachower, Daniel, *The Beautiful Cigar Girl: Mary Rogers, Edgar Allan Poe, and the Invention of Murder* (New York, 2006)

Swirski, Peter, *Between Literature and Science: Poe, Lem, and Explorations in Aesthetics, Cognitive Science, and Literary Knowledge* (Montreal, 2000)

Thoms, Peter, *Detection and Its Designs: Narrative and Power in Nineteenth-century Detective Fiction* (Athens, OH, 1998)

Vines, Lois, *Poe Abroad: Influence, Reputation, Affinities* (Iowa City, IA, 1999)

Walker, I. M., *Edgar Allan Poe: The Critical Heritage* (London, 1986)

Whalen, Terence, *Edgar Allan Poe and the Masses: The Political Economy of Literature in Antebellum America* (Princeton, NJ, 1999)

Zimmerman, Brett, *Edgar Allan Poe: Rhetoric and Style* (Montreal, 2005)

Acknowledgements

Seldom do I have the opportunity to teach what I write, but happily the composition of this Poe biography coincided with the Poe seminar I teach every other year. Since Poe's life and work prompted many lively classroom discussions, I would like to thank the students in that seminar: Lauren Brandeberry, Lauren Burn, Jennifer Canham, Malory Craft, James Dickson, Kara Evans, Cheryl Phillips, Jennifer Pruit, Katie Shinn, Heidi Silcox, William Totten and Drew White. At Reaktion Books, I would like to thank Martha Jay for asking me to undertake this project and for seeing it through the press. I would also like to thank Michael Leaman for his helpful suggestions and Ian Blenkinsop for his patience. As always, I thank my wife Myung-Sook for her encouragement and support throughout the composition of this volume.

Photo Acknowledgements

The author and publishers wish to express their thanks to the following sources of illustrative material and / or permission to reproduce it:

Photos courtesy Library of Congress, Prints and Photographs Division, Washington, DC: pp. 6, 19, 26, 31, 35, 40, 41, 46, 47, 51, 57, 62, 66, 68, 69, 77, 94, 100, 118, 121, 125, 128, 138, 139, 152; frame enlargement from Roger Vadim's 'Metzengerstein', the first segment of the omnibus film *Histories extraordinaires* (Cocinor, 1968): p. 23; frame enlargement of James Sibley Watson and Melville Webber's *The Fall of the House of Usher* (Watson and Webber, 1928): p. 82; Alfred Kubin, *Hans Pfaalls Mondreise und Andere Novellen* (Berlin, 1920): p. 110.